Praise for
OUTRAGEOUS OPENNESS

"This book will change your life. I refer to it regularly."

—Christiane Northrup, M.D., *New York Times*
bestselling author of *Women's Bodies, Women's Wisdom*

"This book offers readers a highly unusual gift—a way to release the exhausting pursuit of the ego's wishes and dreams, a path to living with joy, peace and contentment. Start down that path and miracles begin to happen beyond anything you could have predicted!"

—Marci Shimoff, *New York Times* bestselling author of *Happy for No Reason, Love for No Reason*

"The holy grail is right here in this gem of a book. Look no further for an easeful path to enlightenment infused with rapture and hope, which comes as much-needed medicine for the soul."

—Lissa Rankin, M.D., *New York Times*
bestselling author of *Mind Over Medicine*

"One of the best books we've ever read! My wife, Hollie, and I are huge fans of Tosha Silver. She delivers inspiration on every page!"

—Robert Holden, editor of *Holy Shift!*

"If Amy Sedaris wrote obsessively about the Divine, this is what she might sound like. What a treat."

—Darren Main, author of *Inner Tranquility*

"A fun, fresh spiritual tune-up. Reading it is like taking a bicycle ride or sitting by the stream and suddenly feeling like everything is just deliciously okay."

—Tama Kieves, bestselling author of
Inspired & Unstoppable: Wildly Succeeding in Your Life's Work!

"Tosha Silver's benevolent, heart-expanding book will transform you mightily with the greatest of ease."

—SARK, artist, author of *Succulent Wild Woman*

"Tosha Silver reminds us that the only way to truly live is hand in hand, heart to heart, and hip bump to hip bump with the Divine."

—Sera Beak, author of
Red Hot and Holy: A Heretic's Love Story

"Tosha Silver is an empathetic guide along the ever-present seam between the everyday and the sacred, letting us know that we can pull a thread of aliveness for ourselves at any time."

—Mark Nepo, author of *The Endless Practice*

OUTRAGEOUS OPENNESS

Letting the Divine
Take the Lead

~~

TOSHA SILVER

ATRIA PAPERBACK
NEW YORK LONDON TORONTO SYDNEY NEW DELHI

ATRIA PAPERBACK

An Imprint of Simon & Schuster, Inc.
1230 Avenue of the Americas
New York, NY 10020

First Atria Paperback edition August 2015

ATRIA PAPERBACK and colophon are trademarks of
Simon & Schuster, Inc.

For information about special discounts for bulk purchases, please
contact Simon & Schuster Special Sales at 1-866-506-1949
or business@simonandschuster.com.

The Simon & Schuster Speakers Bureau can bring authors to your
live event. For more information or to book an event, contact the
Simon & Schuster Speakers Bureau at 1-866-248-3049
or visit our website at www.simonspeakers.com.

Manufactured in the United States of America

20 19 18 17 16 15 14 13

ISBN 978-1-4767-8974-3
ISBN 978-1-4767-9348-1 (pbk)
ISBN 978-1-4767-8975-0 (ebook)

Dedicated to Mom and Dad

Contents

Foreword

It's been said that serendipity is God's way of remaining anonymous. So true. The Divine was clearly at work when I met Tosha Silver and discovered how to allow my relationship with God to truly blossom. I was fortunate to receive one of her last astrology readings gifted to me by my daughter. Later, Tosha sent me a copy of *Outrageous Openness*. That was the beginning of my renewed love affair with Spirit. Not only did I read the whole book in one day, finding great joy and relief along the way, I also began to use it as an oracle. Now I keep it at my bedside and open it at random for inspiration when facing a particular challenge. This magical and unique book launched me into a deeper connection with my spiritual heart than I had ever known.

Given our crazy culture where we're taught we've got to be a slave to dogmatic rituals, Tosha's approach is a breath of irreverent fresh air. She describes herself as Plutonic, a devotee of the Hindu goddess Kali, known for her ability to cut through the ego's bullshit and get right to the point. I find this approach spot-on, exhilarating, even hilarious! This chick, a hip tattooed yogini, was an English major at Yale.

She knows how to write prose and poetry that moves the Soul!

Not only did I absorb the book in both written and spoken form like a parched plant that finally got watered, I also joined Tosha Silver's Facebook community, where I soaked up her everyday wisdom. I learned how to offer my life, my heartaches, my problems, and dilemmas to what Tosha calls "The Divine Beloved." This way of relating to God, inspired by the teachings of Sufi poets like Rumi, is reflected in Tosha's message that an intimate, passionate love affair with the Divine is available for everyone.

My own relationship with Divine Order started one morning back in the 1980s. I was reading Florence Scovel Shinn's book *The Game of Life and How to Play It*. Following the instructions, I stood by my bed and said aloud, "Infinite Spirit, send me a sign. Show me the next best use of my gifts and talents." That afternoon I got an unexpected call from an agent I had met several years earlier: "It's the perfect time for you to write a book!"

This was my first direct experience of the truth of Divine Guidance, which is so beautifully articulated in the book you are holding in your hands.

Like most people, I find that I need to be reminded about Divine Order over and over. Because we forget. The ego truly thinks it's in charge. It believes that turning our problems over to a greater power is ridiculous. Our culture is all about hard work and control but zilch about letting go and following the lead of a higher power. After all, there's an acute shortage of double-blind, placebo-controlled studies to prove that offering your troubles to the Divine can work miracles. Yet this is my experience, and that of thousands who have embraced this way of being.

As Tosha illustrates in her wonderfully zany, entertaining stories, Divine Order does not imply that all our desires are instantly granted and we fly away on a magic carpet. Nor does it require that you become passive or colorless, giving up all your preferences. Instead, you become aligned with the spontaneous creative impulses of the Universe in a way that's unique to each person.

In my case, when I got the inspirational call from the agent, I was up to my ears with patient care while also raising my two little girls. I had absolutely no idea how to write a book. How was I supposed to DO that, let alone find the time? Nevertheless, the ideas that led to my first book were saturated with a Divine Destiny. I knew that I was picked to do this job. Along the way, there were big challenges. I had discovered essential information for women that was not covered in medical school or even in my residency. I knew I must create a new positive language focusing on women's health, not women's disease. Despite my commitment, at that time almost no one understood what I was writing about. There was no support from doctors or publishers. Amid all the rejections, only one person, Leslie Meredith, then of Bantam Books, understood my contribution. She skillfully and beautifully midwifed the manuscript and believed in it, every step of the way. Five years later, *Women's Bodies, Women's Wisdom* was published. It went on to become a *New York Times* bestseller in both editions and was translated into eighteen languages. I still get letters from women all over the world whose lives have been changed by its message.

And it all started with a simple act of offering myself and asking for guidance from the Divine.

Knowing that my book was part of a Divine flow helped me keep my faith and stay on course. When God is invited in, it's always a magical experience, and marvelous signs can appear when we least expect it. So, what a so-called coincidence that Leslie Meredith is now at Atria Books, where Tosha's book is being recognized for the true gem that it is, and she too had to travel a difficult road to get here.

With the help of Tosha's amazingly effective Change Me Prayers, I have learned how to truly "Let the Divine Take the Lead" in my own life. I couldn't wait to share *Outrageous Openness* with my community and invited her to be a guest on my Hay House radio show, *Flourish!* After many years of doctoring, I can honestly say this message is the one medicine we all require. Everyone needs a prescription for this universal balm—which has the power to heal our wounds, give them meaning, and release our attachments to what no longer serve us.

I always keep a stash of *Outrageous Openness* to prescribe as needed for those who are ready for it. The relief it provides is truly extraordinary. Tosha's stories are current, humorous, irreverent, and life changing. They're applicable whether you're having a medical crisis or a relationship drama. Her advice that "the perfect solution to any problem is already picked, you will be guided to it in the right way at the right time" has helped me and thousands of others metabolize more stress hormones than any medicine I've ever prescribed. You simply sit back, offer the challenge you're facing to the Divine, and wait for a nudge . . . from a more expanded version of your own self, not some white-haired judgmental guy with a beard sitting on a cloud, waiting to punish us. You're shown what steps to take.

Yes, there are many other books out there about spiritual guidance which are helpful. Then, of course, there are ALL the books about "manifesting." Trust me, I've read them. I've listed my goals every birthday for more than thirty years. I've created countless vision boards and recited countless affirmations. And yet . . . and yet . . . some goals have eluded me despite my efforts. By reading *Outrageous*

Openness and learning to align with the Divine, I've come to know that Divine Order has a bigger plan for me than my limited view. I now trust that what's mine will always come. I gleefully burned all my vision boards. Were they helpful in the past? Yes, but it's even more important to turn those desires over to a Wisdom that is far greater than the intellect can possibly imagine.

Tosha Silver's stories are real, sometimes poignant or comic, but never preachy. This is no dry spiritual tome. It's a juicy, openhearted book, richly woven with fertile stories from Tosha's former career of thirty years as an astrologer and intuitive. You won't find any moralizing here. Just the opposite. She generously shares what she's collected and created through the years: simple and totally profound techniques to help you remember who you REALLY are. This gal knows how to cut through our crap—but she's also a compassionate chronicler of our human foibles. If you're feeling off-kilter, *Outrageous Openness* can be a godsend, a friend who guides you back to center. Tosha shares wise and practical insights to help you remember and align with your higher nature, while still chuckling affectionately or laughing uproariously at the insane world we live in. Immerse yourself in this book, and you can choose a rollicking and intimate relationship with your form of God.

So, I invite you to read this delightful book. Not just once. Not just twice, but repeatedly. Let its message sink into your bones. Soften. Lean back. Be outrageously open to the lead of the Divine Beloved. Surrender into the arms of God in whatever form appeals to you, and prepare to find your life blooming and growing in ways that you couldn't possibly have orchestrated yourself. Watch for the signs. They are everywhere. They are designed to delight your Soul and light up your life in ways you never imagined.

—Christiane Northrup, M.D.

OUTRAGEOUS
OPENNESS

Introduction

The stories in this book are adapted from two years of writing as the *SF Spiritual Examiner* at examiner.com. Because of my long history as an astrologer, I initially assumed the columns might be about how to best navigate current and upcoming planetary cycles. But over time I realized I mostly adored discussing how to align with the Divine, independent of life's endless fluctuations.

I know without doubt that a Force of Love exists that can guide, help, and interact with each of us in the most intimate and practical way no matter what the conditions.

If only we know how to invite It in.

My overriding passion for inviting and dancing with this Force eventually gave birth to this book.

~~~

By the time I began the *Examiner* column in 2009, I had spent twenty-five years giving nearly thirty thousand readings to people from all over the world. Though each situation was unique, the questions in most hearts were similar. "How do I stop worrying? How can I know that things will work out? How can I feel safe?" And often, "Why do I feel so alone?" or "Who am I *really*?" Though there are ways to look at an astrology chart or tarot cards to foretell cycles of relative ease or challenge, I felt that particular information *itself* could never begin to address people's deepest needs and truest longings.

So I began to weave into sessions what had transformed my own life, the principles of *Divine Order and Source* gleaned from reading Florence Scovel Shinn, a writer from the 1940s. Divine Order says that the perfect solution to any problem is already selected if you allow yourself to be guided; Divine Source says there is a natural Universal Abundance that knows how to meet every need. Harmonizing with this Force of Love—call it the Shakti, God, Goddess, One Mind, whatever you will—is the golden key to everything.

If a state of radical openness, acceptance, and attention is held.

Some of my longtime callers were actually people with years of spiritual practice of one kind or another; yet they often felt besieged by confusion, fear, or worry. Even if they meditated, chanted, or practiced yoga, they didn't always have practical tools for aligning with the Divine every day.

Others had either grown up in doctrinaire religions that left them spiritually alienated or were just confirmed cynics on the whole darn topic. But I found that sometimes even the most ironic or skeptical people could use the techniques in this book and witness surprising miracles in the most seemingly mundane areas of life.

Anyone can learn how to move with these Divine principles. Eventually the individual ego's drive to "make things happen" falls away, replaced with a relaxed, trusting openness to answers as they spontaneously arise. These tools are truly accessible to anyone and grow markedly stronger with practice. Synchronicities and magic unfold with more and more frequency, strengthening one's innate trust in the process.

One only needs to be willing to be
Outrageously
Open.

Chapter One

SEEING THE WORLD AS YOU

R V My Mother?

*Don't drink at the water's edge, throw
yourself in. Become the water. Only
then will your thirst be quenched.*
—Jeanette Berson

Years ago I became fascinated by an adorable book called
Are You My Mother?, the tale of a baby bird searching the
world for its home. I wasn't exactly part of its target audi-
ence of teething toddlers.

But because I live at the mercy of an endlessly metaphor-
ical mind, the book held an unexpected appeal. As a lover
of the Divine Feminine, I read it as a story of the Goddess
glimmering in everything. Whether it's Guadalupe, Durga,

Lakshmi, Quan Yin, or what in India would be known reverently as the Shakti, I can't help but love the Mother.

I thought how most of us run from spot to spot perhaps unconsciously seeking Her everywhere. We restlessly scan the world saying, "Is *this* my destination? Can I lay my burden down now? Am I safe? Can I finally let go?"

Yet some part of us knows that no person or place in this galaxy of impermanence can ever fully give that refuge. Everything comes and goes, even that which feels the most familiar. All eventually melts back into the ocean of existence like the iridescent multicolored sands of mandalas.

Amidst this endless phantasmagoria of change, it's possible to learn to rest upon the Divine like a life raft in deep water. From the One all things emanate; to the One all things return. Rather than cling to each individual illusion of safety, the mind can learn to find the Divine and Her protection in every situation.

It's tempting to try to make a particular job, livelihood, or relationship our salvation. Then we quickly become the slave of whatever we grip the most.

But when you make the Divine your Source, you move through life with an ease and lightness, with an open hand. You allow whatever wishes to come, come. And whatever wishes to go, go.

Every gain, and loss, has an odd kind of Providence.

So everything and everyone can indeed become . . . your Mother.

What if God Were All of Us?

What if God were one of us, just a stranger on the bus?
                                              —Joan Osborne

The sidewalks are littered with postcards from God.
                                              —Walt Whitman

I once was approached by one of those online companies that send out daily spiritual messages. You know the kind. Each day you'd get a pithy paragraph about peace or contentment or meditation. They were hunting for new writers and had somehow found me.

So their editor asked for some sample postings, and I obliged. Soon I got back a rather agitated call.

"Excuse me, but what's with all the *stories?*" she asked in a tense voice. "We wanted snappy universal Truths that people can relate to. Our organization is about God, not all these extraneous details. If you want to write for us, keep the personalities out."

But I couldn't. I had loved tales of the Divine in "regular" life since I was a child. I obsessively collected them the way some people do rare wines or Barbies. Any story of a miracle or strange synchronicity held me captive. Over time, the Divine and the mundane had become completely intertwined in my mind. One and the same.

So I answered, "Well, what if God *is* the story? What if the Divine is constantly igniting roadside flares to get our attention? What if there actually *is* a Supreme Organizing Principle with a ribald and unbridled sense of humor? And what if we each have this ardent inner suitor who's writing us love letters every day that often go unopened?"

She said she had to go.

Maybe just as well. Some spiritual groups believe that as we evolve, all the details of our individuality are buffed away into sanitized white-light sameness. Any uniqueness is derided as ego. You see this where members mimic an idea of how to be spiritual; personal style, language, and mannerisms are erased or punished. An eerie, jargon-slinging, one-size-fits-all Stepford-seeker emerges.

And the other route? Well, maybe it's the raucous celebration of God's diversity, just like in nature. The way a lush field of wildflowers bursts open every spring, each type different, colorful, and bedazzled.

Just take a look at saints and mystics throughout history—eccentric and unique as hell, the whole lot. Uninterested in following spiritual rulebooks, they were on fire to know the undiluted truth of their own souls.

Many lovers of Jesus admit he was a straight-talkin'

rabble-rouser who might not have been let into most modern churches. The Indian saint Zipruanna lived on a pile of garbage, while the mystic Lalleshwari wandered through the Calcutta streets half naked and mad with Divine love. The Buddhist goddess Tara was born when a feisty princess was told by monks that she couldn't become enlightened as a woman. She proved them dead wrong and became a Bodhisattva for all time.

So, what if the highest expression of the personal Divine is You, precisely as You are in this very moment, in all your full, authentic, and wounded glory?

Just wonderin'.

Seeing the World as You

*All separation, every kind of estrangement
and alienation is false. All is One—this is
the ultimate solution for every conflict.*
—Nisargadatta Maharaj

Seeing the world as You is a way out of inflated self-importance, or what Buddhists would call "self-cherishing." I've learned about this the strangest way, through my life-long arachnophobia, or fear of spiders. I should call it my slowly-but-steadily-waning terror of spiders.

For as long as I can remember, spiders always paralyzed me. If they were bigger than a quarter, forget it: I'd run screaming from the room like a six-year-old. I can't say the number of times I've frantically begged a friend or partner to come airlift one outside. At least I knew enough to not kill them.

A psychic once suggested that in a prior life I died in a whole vat of them like something out of Indiana Jones. Charming image. And really, who knows?

Some years ago in India I was at a special fire ceremony for Lakshmi, the revered Goddess of beauty and wealth. At one point, a spider the size of a kumquat scurried over my hand. I gasped and swatted it away.

One of the Hindu priests nearly boxed my ears off. "What are you doing?" he yelled. "Mahalakshmi Herself was giving you Her *darshan*, Her private blessing. Are you *insane*?" Then he turned to another monk and muttered, "I *told* you we should never let the idiot Americans come to this stuff."

Well, this got me thinking.

Here I am projecting all my fear on this poor creature, and here She is, the Goddess herself, coming to bless.

What if *She* is a disowned part of *Me*?

I prayed intensely to be healed of my fear.

I was in bed one night ready to turn out the light when suddenly I saw a golf-ball-sized spider on the wall.

Terror, sweat, pounding pulse.

Then I thought, "Hey, why not just *talk* to her?"

"Look," I started, haltingly. "I'm delighted to have you visit, and even come so auspiciously into my bedroom." I took a long deep breath, trying to calm down. "So just let me promise from the get-go, in case you're worried about this all yourself, I *won't* hurt you. I finally know who You are." I gazed at her with as much affection as I could muster for something that had filled my nightmares forever.

Then I continued, "But let me be honest. You really,

really scare me. And you know, I actually wonder right now if you might be a bit scared, too?" This idea actually calmed me down considerably.

I took another breath. "So I'll tell you what, my adorable Goddess. It's a big room. How about if you take the ceiling, I'll take the bed. You just stay up there, my darling multilegged Love, and we'll share a beautiful night."

Perhaps it was chance, perhaps not. But at the exact moment I finished, she began to race up the wall and slip into a dark corner of the ceiling. She tucked in her legs and became a nebulous shadow I could barely see.

I bid her a good night and peacefully fell asleep.

In the morning she was gone.

Later that day I received an email from my friend Erin. On a whim, she had sent me a column she had just written . . . on arachnophobia.

She said it came from fear of one's own power.

I mean, really.

Is anyone ever out there but our Self?

Reincarnation, Love, and Jesus

There is some kiss we want with our whole
lives, the touch of Spirit upon the body.

—Rumi

The idea of past lives has always just made practical sense to me. How else can we explain why a person or place feels overwhelmingly familiar from the start? Or how phenomenal talents emerge with no training? How could Mozart compose sonatas at age seven? Or a little girl in London sing arias almost without training? And how could a New Yorker I know "feel" her way around Paris from day one without a map?

I gave a reading once to a Japanese woman who grew up consumed by the tango. As a child outside Kyoto, she found a sultry album that saved her sanity. Moving to Argentina in her twenties to study, she then traveled the world as a dancer and teacher. I remember her saying, "My torrid, passionate Latin soul was birthed in wet, cold Japan."

All of which explains my love affair with Jesus.

13

Here I am, from a fine, upstanding Jewish family replete with three uncles and three cousins who are rabbis, but I've always had an abiding, fiery love for Him. Mind you, I never wanted to convert to Christianity—or any other religion for that matter.

I just loved Him.

I watched *Agnes of God* in a Greenwich Village movie house many years ago. In an extraordinary scene still seared in my psyche, Meg Tilly took her novice vows, lying on the wooden convent floor to ecstatically intone, "*I am the bride of Christ, I am the bride of Christ.*" I can still see her round shaved head, her glistening gold wedding band, her dark robes. The next thing I knew I was uncontrollably shaking, sobbing, flooded with memory. How else to explain but past lives as a nun?

Hell, I grew up with Hebrew school three times a week and was even bat mitzvahed, yet there I was, the love of Jesus ripping through me in that theater like a cyclone. I was crying so hard the woman in the next seat shot me a dirty look and moved her row.

So every Christmas I decorate a small silver tree in my living room with tinsel, popcorn, and twinkling lights. That alone would have been quite the *shandah*, or scandal, in my childhood. And every Good Friday, I sit for hours in Grace Cathedral in San Francisco. When this holy day coincides with the sacred week of Passover, I walk afterward to David's Deli down the street for chicken matzoh ball soup.

But my heart is on that cross.

However, it's also with the Buddha, Lord Shiva, Ganesh, Kali, the Shekhinah, and every other resplendent, scintillating, riveting, mesmerizing, intoxicating form of Divine Love I am drawn to each day like a flame.

So I kiss the statues on my altar and bathe their little feet in rosewater. I make them tiny necklaces of amethyst and pearl. I feed them almonds, oranges, and sometimes even Schezwan Chinese food.

You see, when it comes to God I am utterly, completely, and madly polyamorous.

And to tell you the truth, I just don't think Jesus would mind.

Not at all.

Chapter Two

SHOPPING WITH GOD

Trying to Function (without God)

Learning to surrender to a very sophisticated Deity
has been the single most important lesson of my life.
—Shirley MacLaine

Lose your inhibition, follow your intuition,
free your inner soul, and break away from tradition.
—Black Eyed Peas, "Let's Get It Started"

When I was in ninth grade my friends and I played a certain game for months on end. No matter what someone said we just added the words "during sex." Such as, "She loves to eat anchovy pizza (during sex)." Or, "He always forgets to do his math homework (during sex)." For whatever reason, this never failed to send us into gales of hysteria.

But then, we were fourteen.

Now I find myself in a new version. Have you noticed how some people will rush to discourage a certain goal? Or at least let you know how futile, exhausting, or expensive your attempt will be before you even *start*?

So in my revised game I always take their words and add "without God."

As in, "It's impossible to find the right job in this economy (without God)." Or, "You'll never be able to find parking there (without God)."

I can't tell you how well this works.

~~

I happened to turn on NPR one day during a mind-boggling interview with an "efficiency expert." He had written a book on procrastination with forty-four "critical steps" to be followed in his *Act for Success* plan. I was soon giggling so hard I had to pull the car over at the corner of Clay and Divisadero just to be safe. Even the poor interviewer sounded flummoxed.

He asked, "So you're telling our listeners they must follow *all* forty-four steps?"

"Absolutely. Every single one," the expert intoned, "in the *proper* order. Otherwise it will *not* work." And he began to fire off the list again.

My head was spinning like a bad carnival ride.

"Well," said the interviewer. "To be honest, that's all a bit daunting. Isn't there a simpler way for people to begin?"

"No." said the expert gravely. "As a master, I devised this plan scientifically. And of course, if people are confused, they should take my seminar."

Of course.

Wiping away tears of laughter, all I could think was "Yep. He's a master of how to overcome procrastination (without God)."

I remembered how life was indeed a weary road before I let the Divine lead the way. I ran from one self-styled "master" to the next with my problems. The combination of a delicate nervous system and a good dose of ADD made my life often derail.

But at some indeterminate point, perhaps more from exhaustion than evolution, I pretty much gave God control. And though problems still come, solutions usually follow in fresh and novel ways.

The other day I met an interesting writer in a café. We started discussing the book proposal I'd been stuck on.

She offered, "Well, I could help you do it. These usually take about thirty hours to create and I charge $250 an hour."

"Wow, are you kidding?" I gasped, doing some quick calculations. "That's over seven thousand dollars!"

"Well, I do have a handy flexible payment plan," she said.

Then I remembered.

That's what a book proposal costs (without God).

When I demurred and left, I sat in my car and invoked Divine Order with my full heart:

"If You wish this written, I cannot do this on my own. You know my limits. But the perfect route is already selected, so if this is Your Will, fling open the doors. If this is meant to be, please bring the right help."

Within a month a writer friend of mine in New Mexico serendipitously emailed me one of her own proposals.

"Hey, you popped into my mind tonight," she wrote. "In case you're still working on that thing, just use mine like a map. You'll finish in no time."

She was right.

The Inner Sherpa

Unexpected travel suggestions are
dancing lessons from God.
—Kurt Vonnegut

Whenever I can, I love to be receptive to how the day wishes to unfold without any planning or interference of the mind. Since this skill grows with practice, I'll intentionally create situations that involve relaxing and letting my instincts guide me. Especially during stressful times, offering a few hours for the subconscious to take over and meander is as relaxing as a two-week holiday.

So here's an adventure I love. I take the ferry to San Francisco without a plan for the afternoon, turn off my phone, and just start walking. The Divine's in the lead. I've done this as a spiritual practice for years now, once or twice a month. I figure we would make a date with a friend or a new love interest—why not make one with the Inner Lord?

Intuition reliably takes over and directs the outing once it's given a chance. Each journey is different, depending on the needs of the time. I usually say a prayer at the beginning: *"I offer this afternoon over to You. Please bring what's most healing and necessary."*

Every short trip has been unique. On some, I felt vigorous and animated, climbing every hill in sight up to Twin Peaks. On others, I sat on a bench staring at trees and feeding birds, craving blankness. Sometimes I ran into long-gone acquaintances and had impromptu meals. Other afternoons were completely silent without even my iPod.

What matters is letting the psyche unfurl without editing or interruption.

Always at the end of these aimless journeys comes a sense of total revitalization, as if my soul got to stretch and relax completely, like a racehorse given a good run. Creative inspirations and solutions to convoluted problems arise of their own volition.

Cheaper than a trip to the Himalayas or even a yoga retreat, right outside your front door, the Divine is waiting to be your afternoon friend and navigator.

Why not invite It?

The Mortgage Meltdown

Cast thy burden upon the Lord.

—Psalm 55

My friend Lori rents an apartment in San Francisco and also owned a house in Northern California. As the economy began to spiral last fall, she started emailing me frantically about selling her home.

She took the same desperate approach to her finances as many people do. Every day she figured her chances of selling got worse as the recession deepened. As she saw the value of her investment decline, she descended into increasing panic. Each time she checked the numbers on Zillow she needed a Xanax.

I suggested she not imbibe the general fear and scarcity of the culture and keep her energy anchored in the Divine as her Source. If she did, her place would sell if it was meant to, regardless of the current market.

~~

Here are the steps:

Release a personal focus. Stop fixating on how much you will win or lose. Instead, invoke a situation where you and a buyer can both win. Imagine the house as a resource you have to offer for the good of all.

Call in Divine Order. Affirm that the perfect new owner is already selected and will arrive easily. Know that you will receive the Divinely appointed price from the right person at the right time, imagining someone who will genuinely benefit.

Install the Divine as the true owner. After all, where did the house come from in the first place? Did it ever truly belong to Lori? At least give God the credit and mentally return the home to the Divine for resolution.

Become detached. Let go of any grasping for outcome. Let go of any attachment to the place or it will block resolution. Detachment creates room for creation. If it's hard to detach, pray to be able to let go and receive the highest outcome. Know that one way or another, no matter how things currently look, God is your Source and you are safe.

After Lori and I spoke she felt a strong impulse to run a real estate post on Craigslist.

Every day she invoked Divine Order and affirmed that the perfect buyer was already selected. She also decided that if the Universe wished her to keep the house, the funds to do so would manifest. She became totally detached, insisting that either way the Divine was in control and she would be fine.

Two months later she sold the spot, without a broker, through that one crummy online ad, to a grateful couple with a new baby for precisely the amount of money she needed.

Let the Leads Arrive

Beside every blade of grass is an angel
saying, "Grow, grow, grow."
—Kabbalistic saying

Last week a Brooklyn businesswoman called me for one of her occasional readings. I always like sparring with Jenna's quick-witted, combative mind. As usual, we reached a point where she insisted that I'm crazy to rely on the Divine.

"It's kinda delusional, don't you think?" she asked. "If there even *is* a God, why would He fritter away His precious time with junk like whether I get a parking space? And would this Force really give a hoot whether I eat veggie or cheese enchiladas? Don't you think He might be busy with genocide?"

Well, if we hold an old-school model of God as the bearded guy in the sky with a Charlton Heston voice and a hectic schedule, then yes, Jenna may be right. But if the Divine is an unlimited Force of Love both within and without us, then why wouldn't we be assisted with even the smallest stuff? Since we ourselves are part of that Force, why wouldn't a flow of help be constantly arriving?

If we are open.

I'm always amazed how even people with meditation practices of many years can resist this Divine aid and direction. And really, what good are all the courses, initiations, and headstands if in the end, the ego does the leading?

I once got an anxious call from someone who had been a director of a meditation retreat for twenty years. She was hurt and angry that she had recently been let go. Even after all that time running a spiritual center, she admitted she had trouble trusting that God might have an alternate plan for her. When she finally laughed at the supreme irony of it all, her panic subsided. She agreed to call in Divine Order.

That night she prayed,

"My perfect new path is already selected and will arrive at the right time. I'll be shown the steps to receive it."

She later emailed to say leads were already arriving for her to follow. One involved traveling to India, a longtime dream and impossibility during her rigorous job.

So here's an experiment. If something's been plaguing you, don't strong-arm a solution. Call in Divine Order.

Allow that the right solution is already chosen and you will be guided to it effortlessly at the right time.

Then let go.

Follow the steps as they appear.

You'll be shown the way.

Shopping with God

> *Pronoia is the suspicion that the whole world*
> *is conspiring to shower you with blessings.*
> —Rob Brezsny

Here's another experiment. Move through a given day, see-ing the world as a living, pulsing, loving Force longing to assist you. Feel that you and this energy are One.

A good prayer can be,

Today the Divine will show me the way. I'm open to
all messages, signs, and omens. I'll move as if there's
a Force of Love waiting to aid me in every area of
my life, big or small.

I often feel I get Divine help with trivialities, so I have faith when the big-ticket issues come, too.

~

Once I had only a few hours to find a dress for my cousin's wedding. And I had just come back from traveling, so I was on a tight budget.

Immediately I invoked Divine Order, *affirming that the perfect dress was picked, and I would be guided to it easily and effortlessly.*

Then I watched my body's impulses.

Soon I felt unexpectedly but intensely drawn to that clothing emporium straight from the seventh-rung-of-shopping hell, Ross Dress for Less.

(Actually, if you *really* want to master shopping with God, just *go there*. Once you've trounced Ross, you're ready for anything.)

When I walked in, the checkout line snaked to the back of the store and on forever. Discarded clothes covered the floor like the scene of a shipwreck. Babies were bawling. Someone screamed at a cashier for a refund. Celine Dion promised loudly over the speakers that a new day was coming. I persevered, clinging to Divine Order like a life raft.

Ten minutes later I spied a wadded-up abandoned dress on a counter. Sleeveless, raw purple silk, short, a little sexy, my exact size. A Donna Karan marked down in true Ross fashion from $175 to $19.99.

Sold!

As I walked to the never-ending line, three more registers suddenly opened. While I waited, a redhead behind me with a sweet smile said, "Wow, totally hot dress. Want these? They're the exact color!" and shoved a pair of dangly earrings in my hand.

In and out in twenty minutes.

Moving through the world open to constant help gets easier and easier with practice. Yes, some days it's much more subtle, some more dramatic. But why not *try*? You could practice this for a full twenty-one days to let your brain waves reset into the new pattern of thinking. And anyway, if you're not happy with the results you can always have your cold dog-eat-dog lonely galaxy back, no questions asked.

Full refund.

People often act as if there's no Divine assistance.

Why not pretend that there *is*?

Chapter Three

WHEN YOU KNOW THE ONE, ANYTHING CAN COME

The Divine Uni-Source

Why worry? What is meant for you
is always meant to find you.
—Indian poet-saint Lalleshwari

The idea of Divine Source seized my life for good reason. Though I was born with an anxious nature, I knew my panic never helped anything. In fact, my whole adrenal system was eventually collapsing like a house of cards from the stress.

Then about twenty years ago I discovered a gem from the 1940s, *The Game of Life and How to Play It* by Florence Scovel Shinn. From this old-fashioned, quirky book I absorbed all I could about Divine Order and Source.

While Divine Order says the perfect *whatever* is always picked and you will be guided to it if you align yourself, Divine Source reminds that *everything* emanates from the One. If you know how to keep your vibration high and attuned to the ultimate Origin of All, whatever is needed can always occur.

You learn to get out of the way, follow the signs, and invite the highest outcome. You stop manipulating results. Synchronicities become rampant. It's like flying above the turbulence in a plane where the air is clear and open, or drinking water from a pristine river rather than begging for it door to door. You start to trust where the flow is going and how to move with it.

It may sound crazy, but if you think of the Divine as your ultimate protection, the Source for your work, finances, and all needs, then even the economy becomes irrelevant. You lift your vibration above the turbulence of the *apparent economic reality* into the hands of that *from which* all things come. No person, place, or thing is seen as your foundation.

Only God.

Then the Universe can use *anything it wishes* to meet your needs. You're no longer limited to what your conditioned mind thinks possible.

Last summer I had an eerie, insistent feeling of suspension. I felt lost and rudderless in a way that is most unusual for me.

So I asked the Divine to send a sign. *Please just show me what I need to understand right now to have faith,* I prayed.

Then on a sweltering August afternoon, I was visiting Calistoga, a small California spa town. Suddenly I noticed a long striped gray snake wiggling down the street next to me, not your usual traveling companion. Tourists wandered by, oblivious. It was as if she was only there for me. We moved together for a block; each time I stopped, so did she. I felt a deep longing to touch her, but she slipped quickly into a crack in a fence when I reached down.

Two days later I was back home in Oakland when a beautiful Asian man with piercing eyes approached. I was shocked to see a large python the color of emeralds slithering around his arm.

"Would you like to pet her?" he asked with a mesmerizing smile. I stood for a long while, letting her slink across my shoulders as she flicked her tiny forked tongue. Since the snake is a Scorpionic symbol of death, rebirth, and the Shakti Herself, I felt instantly calmed and reassured.

My answer had arrived *twice.*

If I just let go and allowed the old skin to shed, rebirth was coming. I would be unavoidably guided to the next chapter at the right time.

I was driving across the Bay Bridge yesterday thinking

about all this when a huge white truck began driving beside me. If I sped up, he sped up. If I slowed down, so did he. I started to wonder what the heck was going on until I glanced over and saw the truck's name: *UniSource*. And the massive logo *Experience the Power of One*. The driver smiled at me apropos of absolutely nothing and waved a tattooed arm.

Okay then.

Not even subtle.

When Shysters Strike

By age seven I had figured out if that if I
just did the opposite of what everyone told
me, things worked out quite well.
　　　　　　　　　　　　　　—Kelly Clark

Forgiveness is the magnet which draws your
endless good. It wipes clean the slate of the
past to let you receive in the present.
　　　　　　　　　　　　—Catherine Ponder

A guy named Tony got involved with my friend Jane. He
was what my Polish-Jewish grandmother would have called
a "smooth shyster," someone who could manipulate almost
anyone. He worked the rounds of Jane's pals, getting each
of us to invest five thousand dollars in his glitzy marketing
plan. And though he set off as many red flags inside me as
an Indy racetrack, I watched in amazement as I forked over
my cash just like everyone else.

A memorable example of ignoring my gut.

But he really was a pro.

As time wore on, one concocted obstacle arose after another, all culminating in the shyster's vanishing with the money, leaving behind only a disconnected phone.

We all had differing reactions. One guy sped off on his Harley for Sebastopol, rumored to be Tony's new home, vowing to "find him and break both his frickin' legs." Someone else hired a sleuth. People spent weeks on the phone in victimized outrage. But Tony had vaporized.

As for me, while I was naïve enough to be snookered, at least I knew what spiritual actions to take.

I wanted my peace of mind back more than anything.

So I prayed:

"Let me release my karma with Tony by forgiving him and myself. Free me from anger and resentment. You alone are my complete Source for abundance. My finances are fully wrapped in Divine Order."

My friends thought I was a fool to forgive him. But over time as I prayed repeatedly it became easy to drop the whole mess.

About six months later when I'd almost forgotten the debacle, someone called who claimed to be Tony's "associate." He said he had something for me.

We agreed to meet at a café in Emeryville, and I dragged along my scrappiest, most tattooed and pierced pal as a bodyguard. But no need. Tony's sidekick was waiting calmly for me, with a manila envelope filled with cash.

He actually said, like someone who'd watched one too many episodes of *The Sopranos*, "Listen, honey, Tony's scammed all over. I never saw him return nuttin' to no one. But he wanted you to have this. And believe me, he don't know why. To be honest, he's kinda rattled that he took from you."

So here's the deal. If you make God your Source for all financial, emotional, and spiritual abundance, you open yourself to unexpected, unlimited good. Each individual person, place, or thing is just the temporary, transitory form the Divine uses to bring what you need.

I'm certain if I had stayed angry, Tony could never have returned the cash. My resentment would have blocked the flow. Praying to forgive him opened the door.

But it also let Divine Source replace the funds however it chose.

If one supply dries up there's always another.

When You Know the One, Anything Can Come

> *There is a supply for every demand.*
> —Florence Scovel Shinn

Divine Source says that if we attune to the sublime level where all is One, our needs will be met in the perfect way. This is the polar opposite of how most people live, attaching to a particular situation like a barnacle to a boat (and sometimes a sinking one at that).

It insists that even a terrific relationship or job is simply the transmitter the universe is using to bring us our good.

Once you anchor in this awareness, you can stop gripping. You know you'll always be provided what you need at the right time, in the right way. *What needs to stay, stays. What needs to go, goes.*

This awareness simply takes practice, since our crazy culture warns forbiddingly that you will lose what you don't clutch.

Actually it's just the *opposite*.

My musician friend Scott was emailed by a guitar player named Joan whose work he liked. She wanted marketing advice; Scott was happy to help.

Then he realized Joan knew someone that he wished to reach. So Scott wrote and asked if she would introduce him.

Joan shot back, "Sorry. Too busy."

Scott ran over to see me, red-faced and furious.

"Okay, look," I said, "You originally didn't help Joan to *get* anything yourself. You did it to be nice and there's nothing you *need* from her if the Divine is in charge. Perhaps she's just too competitive to share.

"But listen, if you're meant to make this contact, you'll be guided in the right way at the right time. Joan sure as heck is *not* your Source. And hey, let go of resentment toward her or it will block the flow."

Scott grudgingly agreed, rolling his eyes.

He called a week later, whooping and hollering. He had just gone to a club in the Castro where he had randomly met a guy who turned out to be close to the person he wanted to reach.

They were all meeting for a drink the following night.

Divine Order and the Phone Company

*If you say to God, "This is terrible!" God
says, "Terrible? You haven't seen anything."
And if you say, "This is good," God says,
"Good? You haven't seen . . ."*
—Old Jewish joke

In India they tell a story about someone who complains to a guru about the smallness of his house. And the guru says, "Listen, go find a sheep and move it into your house. Trust me on this."

The guy does, which of course makes things more crowded. He returns to be told in succession to add a cow, a dog, a chicken, a calf, until things are totally unbearable. When he's finally half out of his mind, he goes back to the teacher, who says, "Now go home and take away each of the animals."

When the guy returns, the guru smiles. "Now doesn't your place feel big?"

I had this happen. With the phone company.

Each month I'd be amazed at what I was paying for my landline, cell, and internet to be bundled together. With taxes and extra fees, this was not exactly the promised bargain.

But I was even more astounded when an extra $42.95 charge appeared one month from a mutant outfit called Keysecure. The description said I was paying a monthly internet "marketing" fee.

Knowing I had never authorized this, I called AT&T. After ten minutes of being tossed around like a Caesar salad, I was told abruptly to call Keysecure. Trying to breathe deeply, I called. After twenty minutes of blaring show tunes, a stressed-out agent got on the phone. He insisted emphatically that I had authorized the charge. He then played "a recording of a prior conversation" which involved much static and a mumbled female voice sounding strangely like Dolly Parton on Vicodin.

"But that's not me!" I screamed. "Just listen. Do I have even a *shred* of a Southern accent?"

"Well, it's you." he barked, "You just don't remember. You authorized it January 27, so don't get huffy with me. And you'll get another bill next month. Hold." Then he threw me back to *Cabaret*.

As my blood pressure continued to rise, I suddenly remembered Divine Order. How could I have forgotten?

With every fiber of my being I invoked God as my Source and cast the burden of this mess. I prayed

that the perfect people who could intercede on my
behalf would come at the right moment.

My psyche uncoiled. I could breathe again. Suddenly feeling an impulse to call AT&T back, I entered a whole new galaxy.

I was helped by a kind, calm woman who admitted they received daily complaints about Keysecure. She offered to promptly reverse the charges and to do so again if they reappeared. She gave me a new number to call to cancel the account, apologizing in advance that it might take months to stop the billing unless I got "lucky."

I continued to invoke Divine Order with total focus. Then I called the new Keysecure number, praying as I sat on hold through the most terrifying version of *Sound of Music* ever made. This time someone answered who cheerfully and instantly deleted my account.

And like that guy in India, my phone bill now seems like a total bargain.

The Cosmic Tip

When you refuse help, you sometimes
refuse people the pleasure of helping.

—Anonymous

I was in a health food store that had a massage corner for short sessions. An unassuming woman sat there with a sign saying *Five Minute Free Trial*.

How could I say no?

As I sat down she said, "You know, this place has been really dead all morning. I'll do fifteen minutes as a gift."

It turned out she was really, really talented. (I should know. Many years ago I was a bodyworker, too, after nearly giving my parents ulcers by choosing massage school—rather than law school—straight from college. But that's a story for another time.)

She gave me such an incredible head and neck massage, I wanted to give her a big tip.

But she was insisting, no, no, it was a gift. Embarrassed by my praise and gratitude, she explained, "I'm a giver, not a receiver. Even though I do so many massages a week, I never get them myself."

Well, I could hardly believe this. She had the sweetest, most healing energy; yet she didn't feel worthy of a compliment, a tip, or even a massage.

Years before, I used to be that way, too. "But it's not hard to change," I told her. "You can inwardly say, *Every day it becomes easier to receive.* Your subconscious will believe this whether your rational mind does or not. You can even pray, *Let me feel worthy to receive what's meant for me.*"

"Besides," I chuckled, "if the Universe *wants* to give to you, why make It work so hard? Who are *you* to say 'no'?"

She gave me a dubious, sideways look as if a mildly entertaining, chatty alien had just teleported to her side.

I didn't mind.

I thanked her again and wished her well. Five minutes later she ran after me in the parking lot.

"You know," she said, her face alight. "I've really, really *got* to change this. I'm not kidding. I *need* to receive." She held out her hand. "So, thanks! I'll take that tip!"

We both started laughing.

"Good thing," I said, fishing my wallet back out, "because I really needed to *give* it. Now will you please put it toward a massage?"

She smiled. "I'd love to."

Chapter Four

FOLLOWING THE INNER LEAD

Think Inside the Box

Bidden or unbidden, God is present.
—C. G. Jung

A problem cannot be solved by the same
level of consciousness that created it.
—Albert Einstein

I grew up a perpetual worrier, perhaps from having a sensitive Pisces mother who always anticipated the next disaster, or from being an East Coast Jew. In any case, by the time I turned twenty-five I was literally making myself sick with fear.

To survive myself, I *had* to change.

One of the first techniques I learned was the God Box. You simply write down your worries and pop them into some kind of container, as simple or elegant as you wish. Whenever a new worry comes up, into the Box it goes. You don't even need a clear concept of God to do this. You could make the offering to your own highest wisdom or to the Force that keeps the birds aloft in the sky. Doesn't matter.

Sounds simplistic, but honestly, it works. If the problem torments you again, you remember, *"It's in the Box. It's done."* You can also add as many other problems as you wish. Because studies show the mind recalibrates in twenty-one days, try to reliably submit a particular worry for at least that long.

During the period of offering, solutions often spontaneously arise. When the mind is no longer grasping for an answer, space opens. The Box gives room for a Divine plan, even in impossible messes.

I first used the Box when I was crazily looking for a new apartment one summer. Friends kept helpfully reminding me that the vacancy rate in the Bay Area was at an all-time time low of 3 percent and that the odds of finding a decent, affordable place were next to nil. But the teacher who had suggested the Box insisted that odds and percentages didn't matter one whit. What matters was the *offering*.

With a sense of bemused curiosity, I scrawled my first note and slipped it in: *"I am now being guided to the right apartment at the right time. It's already handled."*

Within a month my veterinarian asked offhandedly as she checked my kitten for ear mites, "You still need a spot, right? I know one."

She was right; fifteen years later I'm still there.

After a while you start trusting the process. You realize the details of the solution are irrelevant since those will be revealed. What matters is offering the problem over with a sincere, consistent heart.

The Box is also a perfect complement to Divine Order, allowing you to have a sacred place to store your prayers and statements if you wish that. For some practical-minded people, having a concrete spot really helps.

So what do you have to lose but anxiety?

Whisper to a Scream

*The city of truth cannot be built on the
swampy ground of skepticism.*
—Albert Schweitzer

*The god that atheists don't believe
in never existed anyway.*
—Anonymous

One of my unlikeliest but closest friends is Don, an eco-
nomics professor at a local university. He's as skeptical
and left-brained as they come. He likes to introduce me as
his "wacky, psychic pal with the degree from Yale," like a
seven-toed lizard, a two-headed Chihuahua, or some other
freak of nature he happened to find in a corner of Golden
Gate Park.

Once we were at a Berkeley café when he started his latest round of teasing about my "Alleged Close Encounters
with the Divine."

I grabbed his hand and looked in his eyes. "Really, Don,
total truth. Has anything ever happened that made you

wonder if you had the full picture? Anything ever rock your perfect little rational world?"

And he told me that in college he shared a dorm with his friend Joey. One night during a snowstorm, Joey left and hadn't returned by the time Don went to sleep. Nothing unusual.

Suddenly at 3:00 a.m., he awoke with a pounding heart, clearly hearing Joey scream his name. Loudly. Twice. But no one else was in the room.

Half-asleep, he yanked on his clothes and stumbled into his VW bug. His subconscious took over as he slowly drove through a thick blanket of snow. He was drawn like a magnet ten blocks away, where he found Joey's car wedged into a snowdrift. The guy was freezing, drunk, and confused.

No one could ever explain what happened.

I was dumbfounded as I listened, stirring honey in my oatmeal. "Man, you gotta be *kidding*. This didn't change your life at all?"

"No way," Don shook his head vigorously. "I *had* to see it all as coincidence. If I hadn't, I would have begun to question *everything*. I'd been accepted in grad school. I was following all the rules, and winning. No time to rock my world."

"You know," I mused, "I'm not sure that story was a coincidence. You were in the realm of bona fide clairaudience and telepathy. Those are genuine gifts and abilities. Sounds like your Higher Self was making contact."

"Yeh, but I sure couldn't afford to stop for a chat. Next step the loony bin," he laughed, twirling his pointer finger at his brain.

"Well, actually," I said, "in a sane culture this would all be seen as a gift. Children would learn to follow their inner guidance from the *beginning*. Nothing to fear and everything to gain."

"Whatever, sweetheart," said Don, smiling indulgently as he took a sip of green tea. "Maybe next life."

Volcano-Chaser

Move, but don't move the way fear makes you move.

—Rumi

When I was twenty-two and new to San Francisco, I became friends with a writer named Stephen. We hung out in the bohemian Mission district with a pack of other artsy types, feeling at home for the first time in our lives.

After a few months, Stephen suddenly declared that he was leaving the city. He said he was ready to settle down in the countryside, find a mate, even have a kid. Man, did this sound suspect. Like having your favorite gay cousin announce that he was running off to join the Latter Day Saints or the Knights of Columbus or something.

Then he admitted that though he loved the Bay, he was terrified of an earthquake. After spending months hunting the statistically safest place to move, he had settled on rural Washington.

"But you belong *here*," I protested. "How can you leave? You panic even when you can't get a good burrito."

He acknowledged that while he had no real pull to go, he was desperate for a safe home. He knew in astrology that Pluto was coming to his nadir, the bottom of his chart, soon. He felt a major disaster could hit any minute.

"You know," he said, shaking his head sadly. "I just can't live on the San Andreas Fault any more, wondering if my building will still be standing each night when I get home from work."

I can still remember the day we all said good-bye at Nineteenth and Guerrero by his studio. For good luck (and because this was the eighties), we smashed a bottle of cheap champagne on the fender of his peeling blue Dodge.

And then he was gone.

None of us heard a peep until nine months later, when Stephen sheepishly phoned one day to say he was returning.

"What happened?" I asked, elated.

"Well, darlin', remember last May when Mount St. Helens blew for the first time since 1857? And you know that safe haven I had spent so long scientifically picking? I had moved to the town of Cougar, eleven miles away.

"I lost most of my clothes, books, even my ten-speed. Every square inch was packed with ash. I can still smell and taste it all two months later." He sniffled. "You know, I'd *kill* right now for a tofu burrito, extra cheese, guac, and salsa. I swear there's not a decent one in this whole frickin' state. Jeez, I am sooo damn ready to come home."

Stephen returned to the Mission by the end of summer. We took him out to La Cumbre on Valencia, his favorite dive.

To this day he says he's glad it all happened.

He *never* made a decision from fear again.

The Bread Crumb Trail

God only gives us three answers, "Yes,
not yet, or no, I love you too much."

—Anonymous

When I was in my twenties one of my first teachers was a fabulous intuitive in the Berkeley hills named Michael. He gave so many pragmatic tools for how to navigate the inner and outer planes, he saved me years of travail.

Whenever I went to him confused about what action to take in a dilemma, he usually said:

> *"Hold the question in your heart. Ask with complete focus and conviction for the Universe's guidance. Then let go and see what bread crumbs come for you to follow. If you don't get an answer, just keep asking for a while until you do."*

Until I found him I was often paralyzed with indecision on countless topics. With my Libra Rising always seeing both sides of a story, I used to force decisions from fear. But I soon saw that Michael's simple technique worked like a charm.

The variable is the timing. Some bread crumb trails take weeks to appear while things line up. But others are *instant*.

I was driving last week with a friend as she discussed her cat dilemma. She hated that her new kitten from the pound was alone all day, but she feared that two cats would be double the trouble. For ten miles her mind spun like a hamster wheel, endlessly weighing the merits of one kitty versus two.

Finally I'd had *enough*. "Look," I laughed, "why not just ask to be *shown* what to do? Let's call in Divine Order together right now and see."

"Yeh, whatever," she said, rolling her eyes as if I'd just suggested texting Santa Claus at the North Pole.

At the next light, a woman crossed the street. "Oh, my God, girl, check it out!" my friend yelled, pointing. Two tiny calico kitties were nestled in the woman's arms, resting against each other as she headed to the vet on the corner.

"Wow, that was pretty damn quick," I laughed. "Now don't insult the Universe and ignore your answer."

When Credit Is (Over)due

*I never understand when people make a
fuss over me as a writer. I'm just the garden
hose that the water sprays through.*

—Joyce Carol Oates

I'm often thinking about the topic of doership and who in fact is the One "doing the doing." Life changes radically if you know you're a conduit for what wishes to happen as opposed to the one making it all occur.

Then you can inwardly say,

*Use me, whatever I have to give, for the highest
good. Just let me be helpful and contribute my all.*

Over the years, I've watched as that simple prayer has brought people whole new callings and destinies. Once the focus moves from "getting and doing" toward being a vessel, everything changes.

I heard a story once about a spiritual teacher from

France who was a charismatic speaker with the uncanny ability to connect people to the truth of their own hearts. In the beginning, she was deeply grateful to help.

As years went by lecturing around the world, she received much praise and renown. She was treated with tremendous deference and respect, hearing constantly how talented she was.

Then one day she was about to speak in Australia at a huge convention. The conference center was packed; the crowd buzzed with excitement.

She walked to the microphone and opened her mouth.

Nothing came out.

Her voice had vanished.

She spent the next three months essentially mute. This was no common bout of laryngitis; no doctors or tests could diagnose the problem. Her tour was canceled.

Finally she prayed with desperation to understand, feeling like she was losing her mind, not to mention her livelihood.

That night a vivid dream arrived.

"So, tell me," she heard. "Who did your voice belong to *anyway*? In the beginning, you knew. Then you forgot. Remember the truth and it will return."

She ended up prostrate on the floor of her bedroom, offering her voice, her teachings, all she had, back to the One that had silently, patiently, owned it all along.

And a few weeks later it did return.

Chapter Five

GIVING IT ALL UP

The Death Advisor

> *When you make yourself into zero,*
> *your power becomes invincible.*
> —Mahatma Gandhi

> *Let death be your advisor.*
> —Carlos Castaneda

I once heard this story about a friend's sister.

A fortyish woman named Paula lived in Baltimore as a paralegal, busy with relationships, work, family, typical stuff. She was not in the least spiritually inclined.

Then came the shocker. Though she had never had more than a cold, Paula was suddenly diagnosed with a rapidly advancing rare form of lymphoma and given three months to live.

Her world imploded. Practical by nature, she immediately threw her energy into organizing her affairs, handling her imminent departure like one more of the efficient to-do lists that she'd spent her life making. To her amazement, she was not afraid.

Paula paid off her debts, released everything unnecessary, and prepared to die. This world became a diaphanous dream. She ceased having useless conversations. She started telling everyone the truth. She stopped doing anything she didn't want, following her inner clock completely. As she realized this world would go on quite well without her, a peaceful detachment embraced her like a warm bath.

Then, a new twist.

In the third month, the cancer spontaneously left. To the doctors' confusion, all symptoms vanished as fast as they had come. But Paula's calm equanimity remained.

Even more surprising, she had acquired the power to manifest and heal almost anything. If she thought of a certain amount of money, it came almost effortlessly. If she imagined an apple, a stranger pulled one from a bag. People with illnesses began to call for help.

This talent came of its own volition since Paula needed and wanted nothing, having already bid adieu to this world. With no grasping ego, most of her thoughts materialized in a flash. The same Divinity she had once dismissed now flowed unimpeded through her Being.

Paula said, "Maybe when you no longer *need* anything, you can have everything. And when you stop *trying* to make things happen, anything *can*.

"All I know is, the 'me' that used to be is gone. I'm out of the way."

The Secret Bonfire of (the) Desires

What the universe will manifest when
you are in alignment with it is a lot more
interesting than what you try to manifest.
　　　　　　　　　　　　　—Adyashanti

You can come to God as a lover . . . or a prostitute.
　　　　　　　　　　　　　—David Wilcock

Carol, a member of a local meditation group, called for a reading. Every day she was up at dawn to sit, chant, and do Hatha yoga before work. She kept a picture of her spiritual teacher on her dashboard that she gazed at lovingly during red lights. More than anything else, she said she wanted to know God.

Yet she called because she also wanted to know when her "other big desires" would finally hatch. She was on a four-state hunt to bag the right husband. She was on fire for financial success. She longed to own a home, have a few kids. Oh, and be on *Oprah*.

64

So she was saying that she only wanted enlightenment, the Supreme knowledge of her own heart, yet she seethed every day in a cauldron of unmet longings. She visualized, wrote constant lists of her dreams, and made "manifestation" boards with cut-out photos of all her desires.

I went over Carol's transits for the hour then alarmed her by shifting gears. *Why not take her endless piles of lists and boards to the beach and torch the whole lot?* Do what in India would be called a *yagna*, a sacred fire. Offer the whole mess of attachments fully and completely to the Lord of her own heart.

And let go.

After all, she said she wanted God more than anything.

Rather than badger the Divine day and night with her lists, why not pray to receive the highest plan? *Everything could be offered to Divine Order, saying that the perfect route was already selected and she would be guided.* If she prayed only for the Divine Will, the leads to follow would appear at the right time. I've seen this again and again.

When the *Law of Attraction* books became big a few years ago, I began to hear more and more stories like Carol's. Yes, our minds are vastly powerful. We have enormous power to manifest. What we think and anticipate often we *do* attract. But if we draw it with grasping and attachment, suffering will inevitably follow, as night follows any day.

A friend of mine jokingly calls one book "The Secret (to More Karma)."

Yet if you invite Divine Order into all your affairs,
you offer your life to a higher, more sublime Plan,
far beyond the pyrotechnics
of the ego.
You dance through the world
with the Divine Beloved,
knowing that whatever you need,
one way or another,
will always,
always
come.

Always Go to the Top

How long will you keep pounding on an
open door, begging someone to answer?
—Rabia

My friend Cynthia once told me, "Don't waste time trying to get help from people who don't have the power. If you're dealing with a problem, always go to the *top*." Since she'd worked her whole life in the hierarchical jungle of corporations, I listened.

I had been going through a nightmare with an import house. In the course of six weeks they sent the wrong armchair three times, and even double-charged me to boot. Eventually I didn't care about getting the right piece anymore, I just wanted the story over. But each convoluted phone call involved a Kafkaesque voyage into absurdity, being spun from department to department where one unapologetic person after another said they were powerless to help.

So Cynthia advised, "Write the CEO as if he's a friend. He's the top."

I had nothing to lose. I called in Divine Order and asked to be given the right words for the letter. I insisted in my heart that the right solution was already selected. Then I wrote him a companionable but detailed email describing the entire mess. I told every twist in the nutty road and invited his help.

Within a week I had an amused and sincere note of apology with full credit to my account. Even more, he was actually *giving* me the piece as a gift for all my travail. He thanked me for having written.

What a revelation.

I've been thinking how Cynthia's advice applies to the top not only of the corporate heap, but of the spiritual one, too. What if rather than hunting door to door, you go directly to the Divine Arbiter of it all? The gatekeeper Herself of the Cosmic Storehouse?

The One Who is One With You if you are in a sane and remembering state of mind.

That's how I view working with Divine Order and Source. You see the Universe as the unlimited, abundant supply for your needs; you align yourself with receiving the highest solution at any given time. You stop groveling and pleading with others. You detach from *how* the answer needs to arrive and become wildly and totally open to the Divine. You invite the help and follow the route that is shown.

You insist that the right resolution to any problem is already selected and you will be guided. You're open to taking plentiful, even arduous, action if need be. But you know that you will be shown the right routes to follow, and if you need help, it will come.

But first, you know, you do have to make that damn call.

Radical Release

Into Thy hands I commend My spirit.
—Final words of Jesus

I find these words to be some of the most ravishingly beautiful ever uttered. But I'm no Christian (and not much of a practicing Jew either, though I have six, count 'em, six rabbis in my extended family). Over time my spirituality has become an ongoing wildly intimate love affair with the Divine within and without, independent of all formal religion. And this quote says it all.

Every year at the Spring Equinox the sun crosses the sensitive point of twenty-nine degrees Pisces, the last of the zodiac. In the world of the stars, we reach the year's grand finale. When the Equinox arrives, the sun moves to zero degrees Aries, and the wheel of life starts over once more.

This is a day of radical release, ushering us to the brink of the new. Calling this the "crucifixion degree," metaphysicians often warn not to initiate actions at this time.

But I always think if an action is offered completely to

God you can do it *any* time. Strange thing to say as an astrologer who watches the stars, but honestly, it's true.

There's a story that the great yogi Paramahansa Yogananda would request his astrologers to determine the *least* auspicious date to start a world tour. Then he would intentionally begin to travel at that *exact* time to prove that a positive outcome could occur if one moves with God.

In Sanskrit the word *aparagraha* means "nongrasping." Rather than the Western model of chasing, roping, and branding our desires for dear life, aparagraha means moving through the world with an open hand, an open heart. I like it so much I have it inked on my left ankle next to a bluebird of joy.

So here's a good prayer for right now:

> *Let what wants to come, come. Let what wants to go, go.*
> *If it is mine, it will stay. If not, whatever is better will replace it.*

If you fully invoke God's highest will for you, you'll never fear the movement of the stars again.

What a relief.

Chapter Six

BE WHAT YOU SEEK

Your Word Is Your Law

*Thoughts are boomerangs, returning with precision
to their source. Choose wisely what you throw.*

—Anonymous

A strange metaphysical truth: Prosperity is never condi-
tional upon the state of your bank account, but upon your
state of mind. *Matrika Shakti* is the Sanskrit term for the
Supreme power of one's own word. *We craft our world by
what we say.*

Two women called me from opposite ends of the spec-
trum. One, named Marie, was a savvy entrepreneur who
sold an internet company at the start of the tech boom.
Overnight she became a multimillionaire who owned several houses around the world.

Yet she called to say, "Do you know how *hard* it is to live on two million a year? With all my *expenses*? Seriously, it's not much! Every night I seethe in regret that I didn't sell my company for more. I can barely sleep."

I was so flabbergasted I spit my tea all over the phone and had to run for a towel. "Really?" I laughed, wiping the receiver. "Then why not sell a couple of the homes? Does your happiness really depend on *five*?"

"Oh, I *never* could," she protested. "I've waited all my life for them. But no one will believe I'm often *broke*."

She continued to call often to bemoan her resources.

One day I'd finally had it. I said, "Marie, I adore you, but listen. I've never owned a house and I live in an apartment, yet I feel like the frickin' queen of England whenever we talk. I mean, how do I have more than enough but *you* don't? So are you ready to change how you talk about money?"

I didn't hear from her again for a long time. Then she called out of the blue to say she'd declared bankruptcy. Through a series of strange upheavals she'd lost almost everything.

Her word of poverty had indeed become her law.

~~

Meanwhile Lorrie, the other client, lives a modest life, but exists in a true state of grace. Her gratitude and openness pretty much draw whatever she needs. Parking spaces beckon in crowded neighborhoods, extra jobs arrive for extra expenses, loyal friends fall from the sky.

And she wasn't always like this. She used to be a jealous Taurus who seriously resented anyone else's good fortune. But she taught herself a new way to be. She always says, *I have no idea how, but miracles constantly arrive. My needs are always met.*

Recently she felt an urge to travel to Asia but had no superfluous funds. Undeterred, she invoked Divine Order and just waited. She said, *"If I'm meant to go, let the perfect conditions come. Otherwise, let me be content where I am."*

She was cool either way.

The day before she needed to buy her ticket a neighbor called who made films. He asked if he could rent her home for a shoot, offering her the exact travel amount.

Another time, she waited in Manhattan for a bus during a blizzard, sorry that she had forgotten her shawl. Spying a wool scarf a few feet away on the snowy sidewalk, she walked over and put it on, laughing that it was fuchsia, the color of her coat.

The Shakti as perfect stylist.

I've joked that she has so much faith and generosity, the angels compete to help. There's nothing she needs that doesn't arrive one surprising way or another, sometimes in the final hour.

Now *that's* abundance.

Opening to Yes

Yes, there is another world. This is it.
        —Stephen Dunn

"Life can be so unpredictable."
"Well, I certainly hope so!"
        —Becky Sharp, *Vanity Fair*

When a problem has existed for a long time it can feel permanent. The critical, judgmental mind has trouble imagining anything could dissolve such a seemingly entrenched state.

But if you're open, sudden change can happen at any time.

My friend Triana went to a psychic. During her own reading, I somehow came up in the cards. The reader predicted I would soon be writing a lot and finding tremendous happiness in this way.

At the time I found this hilarious. My first thought was, "Writing what? My grocery lists? My movie queue for Netflix?" I might as well have been told I was about to become the new ambassador to Fiji.

Ironically, I'd been dealing with writer's block since college a few decades back. While I periodically scribbled random perceptions on various things, nothing ever came together. I would throw the ADD blizzard of notes that blanketed my desk into an envelope for a vague and ephemeral future. I would stick one more semilegible, chaotic, and rambling journal into my hall closet next to the fuzzy wool blanket where the cats often slept.

Whenever I traveled I would type long, detailed emails to my closest companions. They would always say, "Why don't you start a blog or create some articles? Or write a book? Why don't you share all this?"

But I never did. It seemed *completely* overwhelming. Even corralling the batch of travel letters into publishable articles felt like herding a band of marauding snakes.

So when Triana arrived with her reader's prediction, what could I do but shrug my shoulders and laugh?

"We'll see," I said. "It'll definitely take a miracle."

A miracle.

Suddenly I realized that I had never called in the Divine on this topic! Though I certainly knew better, once again I'd been unconsciously relying on my own limited strength. A guaranteed way to keep things stuck.

So I prayed that Divine Order come into my writing.

I asked that if I could be of service, and if this be God's will, that the perfect chances would arrive to pulverize that damn writer's block once and for all. I insisted that the perfect route was already selected.

I was ready for that miracle. And so, so willing to be surprised.

Three months later I was searching online for an astrology article that had run on examiner.com. I noticed that they were hiring writers. I casually applied.

Soon I was on an unforeseen, wild bobsled run of writing.

Still catapulting madly around the curves and down the ice.

Some obvious things you just can't see coming, no matter *what* you think you know.

The Bliss of No

Don't forget that "No" is a really,
really complete sentence.

—Dita Manelli

My friend Dita mentioned that she had spent the day home from work. I asked, concerned, "Why? Were you sick?"

"Nah," she shrugged, "just felt like it."

I was awestruck by the uber-Sagittarian, offhand way she said that. I might have needed to add, "because you *know* I've been working day and night." Or maybe, "I thought I'd come down with a cold if I didn't stop."

But an elegant, entitled little, "I just *felt* like it"?

Wow.

Exhilarating, unknown terrain for my diligent Capricorn self.

Want to know how hyper-responsible I used to be? Have you ever gotten those pages of awful address labels that charities send you covered with flags or teddy bears or chirping birds? It took me *years* to realize I could just shred that crap and stop defacing my mail.

About the same time I figured out that I didn't have to answer online surveys from my OfficeMax "family" about my recent shopping experience.

And that I saw in a lightning bolt of visionary awareness I could say a quick good-bye when a certain wing-nut relative went on a rabid homophobic rant or two.

I think I was *forty*.

And every day it gets easier.

Sometimes saying no at the right time just makes more and more space for the supreme pleasure of saying yes.

I gave a reading to a well-known novelist named Brynn. She confessed that her Oakland apartment was so crammed with piles of unanswered fan mail, she could hardly move. The overflowing bags, some eight or nine years old, mocked and tortured her. As a dutiful Virgo, she figured if people had gone through the trouble of writing, they deserved a response. But after wrestling all day with one manuscript or another, the last thing she wanted was more work.

I thought mail turning her home into an obstacle course was awfully symbolic. When I suggested that she just bless the letters and burn them all, Brynn nearly wept with happiness. She had wanted this all along.

Brynn wrote to say that after she released the mail her whole life had opened like a sunflower. Her books were her offering.

They were enough.

Be What You Think You Need

The consciousness of "I AM" pulsates through
the entire universe. We attract what we are.
—Teresa Mann

Since I was barely more than a teenager, people have called me with stuff like, "When will a good relationship come?" "When will I have more money?" or "When will I know happiness?" And yes, a decent reader can scry charts or cards to foretell cycles of relative ease or trouble.

But that focus alone really misses the boat. Cycles and transits come and go. They can be helpful to understand. But in the end, what really matters is the right state of mind.

Without a feeling of expansion and contentment, even the blessings from the best of planetary transits won't matter, since abundance is something to be, not seek or await.

If you embody generosity and flow, if you move from Divine Source, what needs to come will always come regardless of the stars or the insane economy. I've seen this so often I no longer doubt. Even if loss or catastrophe happens, it will often reverse.

Sometimes people promise, "I'll act abundantly once the coffers are filled. When I have enough, you'll see. I'll totally share it." Yet here's the catch: You have to act from this expansiveness in your life as it is in order for things to change.

The biblical practice of tithing has power because it doesn't wait for the future. It draws a state of flow into the present by insisting, "In this moment, I have plenty. I'm rich enough to give." If even a dollar is the proper offering, it is enough.

~~

A friend of mine was on the monthly mailing list of an Indian astrologer. She was besieged with warnings of the latest terrifying transits, along with major arm-twisting to buy protective rituals performed by Vedic priests.

Some of the letters she forwarded made my stomach ache, the fear-inducement was so strong. The guy had even found a way to make a nice, romantic Venus transit sound like something to avoid.

Then one day my friend just up and canceled her subscription to the "planetary terror watch." She simply realized she no longer feared the stars. She finally knew that her outer security came from her alignment with God, from a receptive, abundant state of mind.

Each day, regardless of outer fluctuations, she felt:

I Am abundance. I Am love. All that I need always
comes. The Divine is my Source.

She was That. She owned the vibration. She was free.

So give some things away.
Pay for some friends' meals.
Do whatever it takes to feel prosperous
despite current appearances.
And never, ever say you're broke.
If you dwell in the vibration of fear, doubt, and
        constriction
that you will undoubtedly attract.
If you insist you never have enough,
the world will heartily agree.
But if you let yourself be
what you think you need,
one way or another,
it will come.

Chapter Seven

THE HOLIDAY EMERGENCY SURVIVAL KIT

The Inner Tug

People should be more like animals . . . they
should be more intuitive; they should not be too
conscious of what they do while they do it.

—Albert Einstein

Often the next "right" action in life can be felt as a palpable inner pull in almost any situation. You may not know what the correct route will be tomorrow, but in the moment, if you listen, you'll be shown step-by-step the way to go.

With many people traveling during any holiday season, knowing how to honor this inner pull can be invaluable.

I was flying during the Christmas week between Phoenix and Oakland. When I showed up at the gate for my Sunday flight, the airline announced they had overbooked. They were seriously angling for someone to give up her seat in exchange for a free voucher.

But no one stepped forward, so they kept sweetening the deal. Soon they were offering *two* free round-trip tickets anywhere in the States, plus a meal and lodging for the night.

They needed just *one* person, one single person, yet still no takers. Everyone wanted to rush home for the holidays. My inner propulsion to stand up and volunteer was so strong, I practically had to tie myself to my chair with my shawl to stay down. I just knew I couldn't sleep in Phoenix that night.

My mind couldn't understand the power of this inner impulse. I had a class to teach Monday that couldn't be missed, plus a long-awaited doctor's visit. No way could I return home late, no matter how seductive the offer.

Yet I kept feeling this ferocious pull, as if celestial angels themselves were trying to yank me standing. Maybe they were. I finally decided to surrender and trust my gut. But just as I jumped up, another guy rushed forward. To great applause, he became the night's hero.

Twenty minutes later, we all boarded the plane, leaving him to his lonely dinner and night at the airport Holiday Inn.

I was in the last row with an empty seat beside me while we awaited the final passenger. Imagine my surprise when who should come bounding down the aisle but the volunteer himself, pumping his fists in the air like Rocky Balboa. Everyone laughed and applauded once more.

He sat down next to me.

"Hey, what'd I miss?" I asked. "What happened?"

"Dude, just unfrickin'-believable luck," he laughed. "In the final instant, this lady got a call that her cat had escaped. She gave up her seat to go find him. Meanwhile the airline decides to reward me for volunteering. I got to keep the two free tickets, and *still* be home tonight."

I was truly happy for him.

But when the Universe placed him beside me, I finally understood why my body had been pulling me up, despite all logic.

I just hadn't listened.

Signs of the Tide

I've been thinking about how following signs and omens is so central to my life. Since we're all part of a living, breathing, conscious universe, why *wouldn't* it speak to us and give direction?

Why *wouldn't* it send us messages and answers, if only we opened the way?

So to me, operating without the help of signs would be like refusing to turn on the lights in a darkened room. Why stumble around tripping over furniture when the Universe has the bulbs? Yet people can be so busy trying to follow over-amped logic, they don't realize they can just request a sign.

For all the fundamentalist talk that astrology is the

"work of the Devil," the three wise men were guided during Christmas by a *star*, of all things. Some historians even insist that the travelers were clearly astrologers. But then again, contradictions are rampant in the Good Book.

And in many indigenous cultures it's considered precipitous and even disrespectful to nature to move forward without an appropriate sign.

So here's a prayer I've used thousands of times to make decisions. I hold a problem in my heart and inwardly say:

"Please show me your Divine Will in this matter and send a clear sign that gives the proper direction. And if for some reason I'm about to head the wrong way, please, please stop me."

Last autumn I felt a strong longing to be in Mexico for the birthday of the Virgin of Guadalupe on December 12. She's one of those glorious deities I love in all my polyamorous devotional ardor. But on the logical level, the trip didn't make much sense. It was already Thanksgiving, much too late to plan a cost-effective trip.

So I asked for a sign. *Please show me if you wish me to go. If you do, please bring a sign, and a miracle.*

Two days later I was walking in San Francisco and I saw a young Mexican guy wearing a huge Guadalupe T-shirt. Nothing typical, almost like a colorful nightgown all the way to his knees.

"Wow!" I said, "Where did you get *that?*"

"Oh." He looked down and laughed. "I love Her. I went home last year for Her birthday. I was between jobs here so it was like that joke: all I got was this big-ass T-shirt."

When I booked my ticket that afternoon, everything flowed like a dream. A single last-minute frequent flyer seat appeared. Each place I called, from the airport shuttle to the San Miguel inn, offered its final spot.

This also happened once to my client Gigi from Massachusetts. She was trying to decide whether to go to Savannah, Georgia, a town she had never visited, to see their art school. So she called in Divine Order and asked for a sign.

Later that week when she was out for dinner, she kept overhearing "Savannah" from the couple beside her. She soon discovered they lived half the year in her Cape Cod village, and half down there. They invited her to visit.

"After the Universe went through the trouble of bringing them," Gigi told me, giggling, "how could I *not* go? I mean, how random is *that?*"

Ahoy the Psychic Vampire

Listen to your first impressions. They
almost never steer you wrong.

—Anonymous

My first metaphysics teacher used to always give the same advice, "Pay attention to how you feel when you're around someone. And also how you feel when you *leave* them. Pay attention. *Don't question your response.* If you feel bad, simply move away."

My friend Jane recently told me a story. She said, "I was invited to a Thanksgiving meal where the hostess was a talkative, colorful character. While she had a certain charisma, my immediate instinct was to run for the hills. Seriously. The minute I walked into her beautiful, well-appointed home, I felt unaccountably nervous and wanted to leave. But I ignored this sense, thinking, 'How silly; she's adorable and engaging. I must be *nuts*. What's wrong with *me* to feel this?' "

Yet sure enough, as the evening unfolded, the hostess

became more and more drunk and vocal. She eventually moved to be smack next to my friend. And she soon attached herself, like a parasite to a host, to make a steady stream of disturbing comments. She eventually cast negativity and doubt on every area of Jane's life, from her relationship to her work. Jane felt more and more drained and exhausted. She could barely pry herself away to stagger out the door late that night.

Jane said, "Once she got her tentacles in, I literally could *not* move. I was transfixed. It was the damnedest thing. Did you ever see those *National Geographic* shows where an insect paralyzes its prey? *That's* what I felt like. She seemed to psychically know *exactly* how to create my deepest fears."

She grimaced. "It took me a whole day of Epsom salt baths to wash her toxic energy off and stop hearing her inside."

I told Jane she had just been hit up by a psychic vampire. *Big-time.*

And they can be some of the most seemingly charming folks around.

Funny thing was, her instincts *knew* the moment she walked in the door.

But she pushed them away.

The Ease of Flow

Just sit there. Don't do a thing. Just rest.
For this separation from God, from love,
is the hardest work in this world.

—Hafiz

My friend Caren in North Carolina emailed me and said, "Somehow a change has occurred this holiday season. I'm moving from a place of ease and effortlessness, allowing things to happen as they wish to happen."

What a great thought during the time of year when people often become the most fearful and crazed. I immediately wrote the line down. The receptive intuitive mind will absorb the thought even if the critical mind might dispute it.

This idea harmonizes so well with Divine Order. If you align in any moment with the flow of life as it presents itself, all will unfold in the right way at the right time with a certain spontaneity and ease.

Recently I was in line at a grocery in Pacific Heights, buying a few things. An older, well-dressed lady was standing behind me with a pinched, stressed demeanor, her arms brimming with baguettes and brie. I felt an impulse to let her go ahead.

When her whole face suddenly broke into a radiant smile, I glimpsed for a second what she might have looked like as a carefree child. As her food tumbled onto the conveyer she confessed how frantic she felt every year from Thanksgiving on. And how she wished she knew how to be different. "I feel like I hold my life together with safety pins until January," she confessed.

I told her that I had made the decision long ago to feel relaxed during the holidays no matter what.

"Good God!" she exclaimed as if I'd revealed that I secretly had three heads, "How on earth would you do *that*?"

"Well," I said, "I make a thought or two my anchor. Here's my latest one."

I told her Caren's line.

"Ease and effortlessness," she mused. "Oh, I *love* that." Then she whisked out her BlackBerry from her purse to start typing.

"There," she said, "I just emailed it to myself." Then she grabbed me and gave me a hug.

As she walked out the door with her groceries,
her face had opened
like a rose giving its petals
to the sun.

Sometimes, it just doesn't take much.
The most infinitesimal,
unexpected change
can shift
everything

Chapter Eight

WHEN IN DOUBT, CLEAN

The Karma Torch

What you resist persists.

—Carl Jung

My client Julie kept calling about brutal, endless divorce proceedings she was in. She claimed all she wanted was to be done and never lay eyes on her soon-to-be ex again. But she fixated on him like a crazed stalker, even driving by his apartment to peer in the windows at night. She funneled him constant hatred and resentment.

I mentioned that her outrage kept her as karmically bound as when they were first married, even preventing the divorce. Plus, the anger encircled her in a blazing ring of fire that blocked all good, including any new potential partner. How could anyone enter without getting third-degree burns?

Ironically, negative emotions *leash* us to the very people we say we long to escape. They create the likelihood that we will magnetize them back *again* for another round through our sheer attachment, in this life or another. Or they draw new folks who are astonishingly close mimics of the old.

You know, I'm a true spiritual pragmatist. I've forgiven so many folks all kinds of nutty stuff this life just for peace of mind and happiness. Different than condoning hurtful actions, *forgiveness simply sets you free.* It's that basic.

~~~

However, release doesn't always come automatically, especially if the ego has forged an identity out about "how you were done wrong." So here's a plan I shared with Julie. It releases all forms of toxic emotional ties, especially hurt and anger.

Write a letter that won't be sent. Let yourself say absolutely everything you've ever wished to say to this person. Write and write and write without restraint or editing. Swear, scream, defame, curse, whatever it takes. Don't stop until you're really done. Julie wrote over thirty pages.

Burn the letter.

Take a bath of strong Epsom salt water, feeling as you soak that all negative attachments to this person are being pulled from your body and energy field. As the water goes down the drain, imagine everything else goes, too. If no tub, showers can work with a salt scrub.

Burn sage (or any cleansing herb, such as cedar or frankincense). Bring the smoke through your whole body from head to toe, front and back. Imagine any final psychic cords attaching you melting away. They're like ropes of energy that bind us to people. You'll feel them leave.

Release any pictures, letters, or objects from the person that fill your home. Those hold their psychic *prana*, or energy, making it much harder to cut free. They may even reattach cording if you dwell on them. Let them go.

Pray for closure. Ask the Universe to let you completely release this matter. Ask to be able to forgive the past and be carried to a new time. A version of a prayer could be, *"This entire relationship now belongs to Divine Order. It is in God's hands, and I am open to a miracle of completion. The situation now unfolds in the perfect way for the good of all. I needn't fear letting go; my needs are always met."*

Send blessings to them, and to yourself. This one can be tough but is actually the *most* important. See each of you moving on. Be willing to see them at peace. Sending them blessings ironically breaks any attachment once and for all. (And has *nothing* to do with condoning any ways they hurt you. It simply means you bless them nonetheless and are done.) If you feel stuck, you can pray for the willingness to do this. It will come.

Julie had such a force field of fury about this guy she repeated the process *three full times* until she felt complete. A week later he wrote, suddenly agreeing to many concessions he had been stubbornly resisting.

Her new destiny could begin.

The Energy Vacuum

Nature abhors a vacuum.

—Aristotle

In the United States stuff is alive
but the people, not so much.

—Maria, my Mexican pal

When I teach classes in Divine Order, I usually suggest everyone spend the first three weeks cleaning out their homes. And their cars. Even their purses and wallets. When people let go of their clutter, the spiritual work can deeply penetrate.

In fact, I'd discovered, in the early years of teaching, that Divine Order simply didn't have room to fully enter *until people made space.* When they let go of what they *didn't* need, what they *did* could finally arrive.

So each person would create an intentional vacuum.

I remember Gina, a double Cancer, who was a serious pack rat. Every corner of her studio apartment had dusty towers of old magazines. Her closets were brimming with unworn clothes, her drawers with crumpled bills and letters. But the thought of decluttering filled her with such dread she almost dropped out of the group.

She bravely persevered, however, calling upon the Divine for assistance. *She prayed to be shown what to release and what to keep.* If she had relied on her ego to make the decision, she'd probably still have every moldy scrap. The idea of letting go gave her actual panic attacks, even though she was practically entombed in her own home.

By the end of the class, years of old, stagnant energy had been cleared. Some friends volunteered to haul away three full trucks of junk for her. She was amazed how much help came once she became willing to *go for it.*

Now this woman's work and love life had been frozen for so long it was like a cadaver. But soon a stimulating new job arrived, and an old girlfriend she still loved returned—an amazing event. Gina even resumed exercising, which she'd stopped many years before.

She called me one night, ecstatic. "Oh, I get it now. How could the good even have gotten in the front door? It was blocked by all the garbage."

I remember another woman who had an exquisite, rare Turkish carpet left behind by her ex-husband. Despite its beauty, it haunted her every day with memories of their tortured marriage. She would constantly fume, "All I got from that rotten bastard is this frickin' rug."

I laughed and suggested she let it go. When it finally sold at an auction, she became almost immediately infused with an inexplicable buoyancy. She took the money and went for a week to Hawaii. She couldn't believe she'd kept the beautiful, wretched thing for so long—next to her bed, of all places.

~~

I constantly clear my own space out. Yet I have to admit, releasing my archaic *Seinfeld* videos brought a pang or two. But I think I knew every one by heart anyway. Sometimes when I sat down to meditate, that part where Jerry and Kramer put cement in their washing machine would still play in my mind all these years later. So obviously they'd already amply served their high spiritual purpose.

And if *I* could release old *Seinfeld*, you can let go of *anything*. You don't have to release anything you use, love, or need. *Just the rest of it.* Your intuition will show you.

Finally, if you're having a particularly knotty dilemma you can offer the cleaning to its resolution. Recently I was stuck in some old fear and anger. So I simply went into the kitchen and found a messy drawer. I offered its rehabilitation to the Divine, affirming that as the drawer was sorted, so would I be.

A half hour later, I was free.

You use the external form you clean as a template for your inner psyche.

And you elevate a seemingly mundane chore into a most holy offering.

Arsenic on the Rocks?

Run my dear from anyone and anything that does
not strengthen your precious budding wings.

—Hafiz

Set your life on fire. Seek those who fan your flame.

—Mevlana Rumi

I love to offer problems to the Divine so unexpected solutions can blossom. In a sense, welcoming cosmic intervention is like planting a seedling. You put the fledging roots into the soil, and then fertilize and water to allow for flowering. The more you protect the plant, the better it grows.

So would you pour arsenic on that delicate thing to see if it could survive? Would you stick it in burning sun for a week just as an experiment?

Yet often when we're in the midst of sprouting a new life, we continue to engage the negativity and fears of others. Our new thoughts are germinating, our energy is awakening. We need to guard and nourish the new life. It's like putting up a fence around your garden so the raccoons don't rampage your lettuce.

Let's say you've just lost your job, and you're taking all the spiritual steps I've been writing about. You call in Divine Order. You say that the perfect new work is already picked and will arrive in the right way at the right time. If need be, you put your worries about your future into a God Box. You affirm that the bread crumb trail will arrive, the perfect steps for action will be shown. You anchor in Divine Source.

But as this process unfolds, you want to *protect* it. You can't indulge fear and negativity at the same time.

You need time to sprout.

～～

A couple of years ago, I had to have an ovary removed. I wrapped the event in Divine Order, affirming that the perfect surgeon was already picked and that everything would unfold in the highest, most peaceful way. And indeed it did, until two days before.

A phone message came late that night from an acquaintance. She started by saying she was only calling from the *greatest* love and caring. Then she launched into a bizarre recital of the world's most freak surgical disasters that might be visiting my own body sometime soon. She recounted with gusto everything from fatal allergies to anesthetics to a particularly riveting tale of a gal who died when a scalpel was left in her colon by an absent-minded surgeon.

If I hadn't been shaking with fear, I would have been falling over with laughter.

An hour later I saw I had absorbed all her energy. I shook it off, soaking in a lavender bath for cleansing.

By morning I was calm. The surgery went well.

And I learned to not drink other people's poison, even when it's offered with "love."

Chapter Nine

OBJECTS IN MIRROR ARE CLOSER THAN THEY APPEAR

No Worry, Send Blessings

Worry is like throwing kerosene on a fire.
—Suki James

Often in the course of a session, people tell me of someone they're concerned about. Maybe they have a child, parent, or friend with a medical issue or financial problem. They say they worry about this person all day long as a token of their undying love.

But if you care about someone, worry is the worst energy you can send. It directly transmits fear and restriction, since we usually visualize all the darkest possible outcomes.

So even if it's well-intended, worry blankets the poor recipient's energy field in a negative vibe. Imagine a black Express Mail envelope marked "Thinking of You" filled with muck, mildew, and a few skull bones.

That's worry.

So it's simple instead to learn to send blessings as soon as worry begins. Just hold the person in your mind filled with light and happiness, see them peaceful and content. Do it day after day. That's the single most useful gift you can mentally offer *anyone* you love.

A woman called who was panicked about her daughter's first pregnancy. Every night she lay awake visualizing every possible disaster. Her imagination was on overdrive. "What if her daughter tripped and fell down the stairs in her final trimester?" "What if the baby was unexpectedly premature?" "What if one day it hated its grandmother?"

Because she and her daughter were so bound, I knew the young woman was receiving this energy and worrying even *more*. And then imagine what the fetus was receiving. The tiny thing is thinking, "Yo, what *are* you crazy people out there *sending* me? I'm just floating here in amniotic happiness. What is *up* with you all?"

So I convinced my client to send blessings.

I got an email later. She had created a circle of friends and family who got on the phone every night to mentally send her daughter light. They surrounded the birth with ease and happiness.

The daughter began to feel uplifted; the birth went well.

Cynics might say it could have gone smoothly anyway, but who cares? Why make loved ones shovel their way through all the fear you're unintentionally sending?

And if you think you don't have *time* to bless someone, consider how consuming worry can be. Anxiety can be a full-time hyper-focus mental devotion for an obsessed mind. And learning to shift from worry to blessings just takes practice.

So *send* them.

To your loved ones, to strangers, to enemies, to animals, to the planet.

And of course, to *you*.

Metta Meditation: Joy to the World

The root of your problems vanishes
when you cherish others.
—Buddhist teaching

Om mani padme hum.
—Mantra of Chenrezig, Buddha of Compassion

I love the practice of metta, the simple sending of *loving-kindness to yourself and others, including those who are difficult*. I've been planning to write about it for a while. Then yesterday, as I was crossing the Golden Gate Bridge, a bird's-egg-blue van pulled in front of me decorated with pictures of the Buddha. A bona fide Metta-Mobile.

Quite the nudge.

To practice, just sit quietly and follow the breath. Then begin to pour peace, love, and forgiveness, first to yourself. You bless yourself and all you may be inwardly blaming. Then you move on to those

you love, then those you have trouble with, and
eventually encompassing the whole world.

I also use metta in specific ways. Once I was going through
some heartbreak in a relationship. So I focused the blessings
on all the others in the world who were having that, too.
You can easily feel yourself psychically linked to everyone
having the same travail, and send them love.

The whole world bursts open.

Suddenly you are no longer a struggling, isolated being;
you are one with humanity. And as you send blessings, you
become a Divine conduit. You are immediately plugged
back into God as your own abundant Source.

~~~

I needed to mail a box. The line for the post office counter was out the door, but even the one to the postage machine was endless. I could feel everyone's agitation rising
like black smoke. It was hard to not feel the same way.

Then I remembered metta. I focused on my breath and
began sending love to the frustrated part of myself trapped
in post office limbo-hell. My body relaxed; I grew calm.
Then I began blessing the others, pouring love, happiness,
and fulfillment to everyone in the line. A few moments later
came an unexpected shift.

The line was stalled because some foreign speakers

couldn't understand the machine. Suddenly a translator arrived and the line began moving. People all started chatting and laughing with relief.

Now, of course, when you use metta there's not always such an immediate or vivid response. But it uplifts any situation. If a miracle is meant to happen, it can only help pave the way.

More important, you never know how much someone—perhaps the tired-looking, beleaguered stranger standing right beside you—may be in desperate need of *precisely* what you send.

Death Becomes Her

Anything forced into manifestation through
personal will is always "ill gotten."
—Florence Scovel Shinn

One of my favorite books is a deceptively simple tome called *The Game of Life and How to Play It* by Florence Scovell Shinn, a New York metaphysician from the 1940s with a disarmingly direct manner. I loved her instantly. She shared the basic principles of Divine Order and Selection with pristine clarity.

Discovering this text changed me overnight. I started seeing how anyone could learn to dance with life if the mind was kept positive and receptive. The book with the funny, archaic name became my bible.

In one story Shinn told of a woman who coveted a certain home. Every day she visualized herself there, totally transfixed. When the owner finally died one day of a sudden illness, the woman bought the place, thrilled that her dream had come true.

Yet from the moment she moved in, a nightmare ensued, including the unexpected death of her own partner. One day she asked Shinn if she had helped *cause* the former owner's passing through her obsession. Shinn replied, "Quite likely. Your determination to get what you wanted was so strong, you helped the other woman 'leave.' Now you're reaping the fruit."

She went on, "It would have been far better to call in Divine Order and say, *'Bring the home that's right for me. Let Divine Order pick the perfect place that's meant to be mine.'*"

〜

Well, the story scared the bejeezus out of me. I could feel its essential truth. My own strong attachments had often created painful, chaotic results; luckily I was almost spent. Florence's book had arrived like the cavalry.

Rather than blindly chasing outcomes, she taught me to inwardly ask, *"Let things happen as they are meant to, in the highest way for all involved."*

If you ask the Universe to bring what's right, you can't go wrong. I've watched through thousands of readings how trouble invariably follows when someone tries to commandeer what is not theirs. Even the word *disaster* means "going against the stars."

But Divine Order always brings the right solution at the right time. You learn to relax and follow the cosmically ordained route when it appears.

You won't miss it.

Out of the Cosmic Dumpster

> *You yourself, as much as anyone in the entire*
> *Universe, deserve your own love and affection.*
> —Buddha

> *There is a basket of fresh bread on your head,*
> *yet you go door to door asking for crusts.*
> —Rumi

I went through a harrowing period in the late eighties when my endocrine system crashed and burned. I spent the better part of three years mostly on my back, submerged in deep despair. After a year, Western medicine admitted its inability to heal me and helpfully suggested I find creative ways to make a life from bed. "You're still really smart, you know," said my MD at the time. "And you're only thirty. Couldn't you consider this all a positive new chapter and learn to crochet yoga bags or something?"

Little did I know that eventually an inspired acupuncturist would arrive out of nowhere to turn the entire situation around.

But something happened the month before she appeared. In some ways I think of it as the event that *let her* appear.

I was living in a tiny studio in a building in the Richmond district of San Francisco. It was a dismal room with a small fridge and a bath—all I could afford. In my state of illness and despondency, I had gone from being surrounded by pristine beauty to barely washing my clothes. "Why bother?" I would muse. "I'm just in this decrepit cave waiting to die."

In the building's basement was a Dumpster for people's trash. Once a week I voyaged down with all the empty boxes of Chinese takeout I had come to subsist on.

But one day the garbage rocked my world.

Leaning against the bin was a huge brand-new poster of the Hindu deities Lakshmi, Ganesh, and Saraswati in all their resplendent, vibrant glory. Gold shiny glitter glistened on their lush forms.

Well, I had a long, long history with these guys. They had decorated all my apartments until I became ill; they were my soul's oldest pals. I carried their pictures in my wallet the way some people do their children. Yet when my life began spiraling into its nightmarish abyss, I had slammed the door of my heart and spat an angry good-bye. Having given many readings to folks who felt abandoned by God, I sure knew about spiritual betrayal.

Yet there was the whole beloved cosmic gang, patiently and oddly smiling in my basement, still wrapped in shiny cellophane. Waiting. Ganesh's soft, kind eyes drew me like a magnet.

Even in my deranged hopelessness, I knew one hell of a sign when I saw one. I had pitched *myself* into the trash during this dark night, giving up on any faith that the Universe might have an inconceivable plan for me. I'd lost any awareness of myself as sacred or even *worthy* of aid.

I carefully took the poster upstairs and hung it on the bare white wall over my bed. For the first time in months, I thoroughly cleaned the place and lit some sandalwood incense. Then I shuffled down the block to a laundromat, beginning the first of many loads.

The next day I walked across the street to have my hair cut. I told my poor body I was so sorry for its suffering and vowed to be of help.

My recovery had begun.

Chapter Ten

OWN YOUR POWER (OR SOMEONE ELSE WILL)

Nothing Personal

Love and compassion are necessities, not luxuries.
Without them humanity cannot survive.

—Dalai Lama

Maybe it's being born with Neptune on my Ascendant, but I've never understood how to pop everything efficiently into those security bins at airports. I marvel at folks who just calmly take off a couple items and waltz through. I usually have six layers of clothes, a shawl, a laptop, a purse, that damn mandatory Ziploc bag for liquids with half the bottles falling out, and rings on every finger triggering the alarms. Even when I prep ahead, I still seem to need seven bins and more time than a mother with twins.

So this last trip to New York, I innovated. I stepped out of the line, organized all my stuff, and asked a woman if I could get back in. I made a joke about trying out a new plan.

Suddenly her face twisted into a dark mask of anger. She screamed, "Listen, lady. I don't care about your freakin' story. Just get back in the goddam line!" She began to complain in a booming voice to anyone who would listen about my obvious idiocy.

The spectacle was fascinating.

Her reaction was so torrential and unexpected I just gasped.

Then I flashed on how I would have reacted in the past.

Years ago, still at the mercy of my sensitive nature, I would have surely burst into tears, sulked away like a chastised child, and apologetically re-entered the line near someone new.

Ten years later, I might have just matched her fire, smashing back her rage like a toxic tennis ball and telling her to go to hell. An odd kind of progress.

But now there was Door Number Three.

As she attacked, a sense arose within me, "Wow, this poor disturbed lady. She can barely get through the day. This has nothing at all to do with me."

I grinned into her steely eyes and got back in the line. Standing nearby, I could feel the poignancy of her explosion. I had an overwhelming sense of someone who had never been listened to, whose own voice had never been heard. No wonder she was so pissed.

All I could feel was, "This is how she talks to herself. This is how she was treated." I remembered some of that from my own childhood. "She just never knew she could change inside."

Waves of compassion arose as I mentally sent her good thoughts. Then I couldn't help chuckling as I moved on through the line.

For all my attempts at preparation, chaos had found me at the airport once again.

Free the Psychic Hostage

*Thinking for oneself is an opportunity
not to be missed.*

—Yuki Tomo

Sometimes we turn our lives over, not to a Power greater than ourselves, but to an unintentional petty dictator. Then we live in a walking dream as their psychic puppet, even when they're no longer around to pull the strings.

I've had clients who have spent half their lives in therapy trying to understand the grip a particular parent has had on their psyche. But they never fully cut the cord. There's nothing more poignant than someone in their thirties, forties, or beyond who's still an abject slave to his or her past.

While my own father has a huge, generous heart and a fabulous sense of humor, he was also quite demanding when I was young. *Nothing* felt good enough. And though I believe I selected him as a soul to resolve certain karmas, I couldn't fully free myself as an adult from what seemed like his steadily critical voice. While I had so much love for him, a part of me remained his obedient but ever-disappointing child.

Then a few months ago I hit a horrible writing block. A project was almost due. So one day I just prayed in desperation. "Please, please get me out of the way, I need my *own* voice. I need to be enough as I am."

The next thing I knew I felt drawn to the ocean. I brought a letter from my dad that hurt me whether he intended it or not. I honestly could no longer tell what was real or my own entrenched reaction.

Then I stopped at the store for a coconut and flowers. I was set to do a ritual from India I'd performed about other topics before.

It was time to offer the whole mess, once and for all, to the Divine. I meditated for a long while, pouring every frustrated thought and feeling into the coconut sitting in my lap. Then I got up and smashed it against a stone wall, watching the milk explode like a psychic grenade.

Now I needed to burn the letter, but the wind was so strong my lighter was useless. Unbelievably, I saw two young guys a few yards away tending a huge fire. "Am I dreaming?" I thought. "On Ocean Beach in the middle of the day?"

I walked over and explained the story. "Watch out! The heat is *ferocious*," one guy cautioned. "Want me to throw it in so you don't get burned?"

"No!" I yelled, the wind whipping my hair. "I'm the daughter. I have to!"

I grabbed a long stick to plunge the paper into the leaping orange flames. As the pages burned to floating gray ash, the guys high-fived me, yelling, "You're free, mama, you are free!" They toasted me with their Heinekens while one even danced a little victory jig.

Later, I left a trail of purple orchids along the water's edge in gratitude, most of all to my fierce and beloved dad. The wildness of my own fiery, passionate nature came directly from him.

You know, at some point *you* have to free the inner hostage.

No one else can storm the gates.

You *alone* can finally break the barricades and just free . . . you.

On Friends Who Love Your Suffering

People who have let go of their dreams are
sometimes eager to help you bury your own.
—Anonymous

I gave a reading to a designer named Patty who lives near Lake Michigan. She told me about her "bad-weather friend."

"You know how people talk about fair-weather friends?" she asked. "The ones who only come around when things are good? Well, girl, I had the *opposite*. One of my closest pals, Mary, always seemed to love love looove my disasters. As long as I was having a financial meltdown, a romantic breakup, or a health fiasco, she'd be total support. She'd listen forever, nod sympathetically, and cluck about how sorry she felt.

"A couple of years ago when my fiancé left me during the same week I broke my hand, Mary was actually beaming. She was a helpful dynamo, all the while marveling over my life. She trilled, 'Oh, baby, you've just got you the *worst* karma. I simply don't know how you *survive*.'

"I wanted to kill her. And then I felt guilty 'cause she was saving my ass.

"Her help came at quite the price." Patty gave a long exhalation. "But this year I've made a ton of changes. I'm drawing on Divine Order, yoga, affirmations, everything I can. Things are blooming. And Mary, to be honest, is *pissed*."

I sympathized. While you sure don't want friends who vanish when you're in trouble, you don't need someone threatened by your happiness either. The right people would be happy for your joy.

But if people don't believe that the good that is meant for *them* can come, they'll be jealous of your own. They'll believe that there's only a certain amount of abundance in the Universal Bank, and if you receive yours, they'll have less. But that's plumb crazy. It's thinking based on scarcity, fear, and deprivation.

In truth, the happier, more content, and more fulfilled you genuinely feel, the more you have to give. Everyone.

My first psychic teacher repeated something a lot. He'd say, "You can't tell whether someone is good for you when they're around. But after you leave them, see how you feel. Did they fill you? Drain you? If you're consistently depleted, *trust that*. Then cut back or drop them altogether.

"Bless them and let them go."

Drop the Victim

*Revenge is like taking poison and waiting
for the other person to die.*
—Carrie Fisher

The only real beauty is self-acceptance.
—Megan Fox

I gave a reading to Patrice, who was in one of those relationship dramas that are almost a boring cliché. Nearing fifty, she had just been "dumped" by Ed, her husband of twenty years, for a woman half her age. She called me howling like a wounded tiger, filled with indignation and pain.

She was also completely consumed with hating the younger gal. She spent most of her time furious, convinced if "that hussy hadn't gone after her man" all would still be well. And even though Patrice is actually a Pilates teacher who's in unbelievable shape, she felt ancient compared to her nemesis.

Well, I barely knew where to begin.

First, I admitted that while I understood her hurt, I just

don't believe in rejection or competition. In the psychic realm, they're both mirages. If you anchor yourself in Divine Source, *what needs to come will always come, regardless of others.*

(By the way, I'm not ignoring the ageism and sexism that permeate our culture and fuel such sagas. But everyone actually can learn to hold their energy separate from these limiting motifs. In other words, *not buy the lie.*)

As we looked at her chart together, a different story emerged from what she'd said. The marriage had been nearly dead for seven years, going back to her chart's last Saturn square. Patrice at first fell silent, then quietly admitted this was so. She had been feeling trapped for a long, long time. While she and her husband both worked full-time and had no kids, she still handled everything at home, feeling like a cross between a maid, a secretary, and a nanny. On top of that, they never talked.

She had fantasized leaving every day.

"So you got your wish!" I said. "This has nothing to do with some chick *taking* him. No one can steal someone unless they're in an international underground kidnapping ring or something. So *was* she?"

"Not that I know of," Patrice laughed. "But *I* wanted to be the one to leave. And *I* wanted to find someone first, not *him.*"

So really she had been miserable for years with a guy

who was having affairs while she cleaned the bathroom on her days off.

She had long wanted out. And finally the Universe gave her the jail keys.

"One day," I grinned, "you should send your replacement a thank-you note. Seriously. She might end up scrubbing his damn bathtub while *you'll* be free on weekends to hike Mt. Tam."

Admittedly, Patrice is an intense New Yorker who's a really quick study. Like many Leos, once she's done, she's *so* done. She dropped her victim story like a hot coal. She stopped saying she was dumped and decided she was grateful to be released.

And she stopped comparing herself to the Other, pretending that she was beautiful just as she was.

"If you pretend for a while it actually becomes true," I promised. "The receptive level of your intuitive mind believes what you tell it. It's malleable and plastic, awaiting your every word. *Be careful what you say!*"

Eventually she emailed me that she was seeing someone new.

"And get this," she wrote. "Soon after we met he said, 'Do you know how rare it is to meet a woman who seems to like herself as she *is*? You radiate that.'"

Why Give Your Power to a Reader (or Anyone Else)?

*Enlightenment is learning to stand
on your own two feet.*

—Adyashanti

*When you knock, ask to see God . . . not
any of the self-appointed intermediaries.*

—Thoreau

Some days my work life is a walking contradiction. When I'm not giving classes or writing, I've been giving readings since I was practically a teen. Yet I laugh that I'm "The Reluctant Psychic."

Now don't get me wrong—I often enjoy my work. I like acting as a trusted second opinion for people's intuition. Yet I've always been saddened by how some folks are dying to give their power away to someone, anyone. Some wish they could have a reader decide everything.

But a good intuitive never grabs the wheel. She helps

people see a reasonable route and know the pitfalls and lessons along the way. She has them match what they are intuitively feeling with the advice.

Besides, no one can be 100 percent accurate with predictions. Our future is what Sanskrit calls the parabhda karma, the bodily destiny combined with what we create through our evolving actions and thoughts. Learning to keep our vibration high and positive is the key. We make our future anew every day, since life's a mix of fate and free will, with a dash of mystery that could never be fully read.

In a good reading you are empowered, not some quaking victim of predictions. Your deepest intuitions are confirmed as your body feels the rightness of what you hear. While there are definitely good readers out there, there are some to flee, flee, flee. They profit by creating worry and dependency. They stockpile their bank accounts with the currency of fear.

And in any case, I often believe the next "right" step in a dilemma is to call in Divine Order. My true passion is helping people align with the Divine.

～

For years I've read Elaine and Zelda, one of the first same-sex couples to legally marry in LA. They both have powerful, fixed charts, so they have their battles, without a doubt. Nonetheless, the more they turn their union over to the Divine, the better it goes.

Elaine wrote me alarmed that a psychic promised they'd only be together two more years. I asked, "Why would anyone predict this? You just had a baby together, for chrissake. Why create such horrible thoughts?"

Besides, you'd never know if such a prediction would create the event. I calmed Elaine down by insisting that if they called in Divine Order, they'd be together as long as was karmically right. No need to fear.

Fortune-telling be damned.

The same thing happened to my friend Dave, who was dating a guy he enjoyed, just letting the story unfold. Then a reader, unsolicited, shared that the current boyfriend was wrong for him, and a different guy would arrive later. Suddenly Dave could no longer be present; the psychic's words boomed in his brain like a mutant radio station gone mad. I showed him how to let them go.

A good reader can be an invaluable sherpa in the mountains, pointing out which trails work best and helping you find your way.

A bad one can lead you right over the next cliff.

Don't blindly follow.

Your answers are inside you.

Chapter Eleven

ROMANTIC KISMET

Marrying Kali

A heart does not choose.

—Colette

But it just might be a lunatic you're looking for.

—Billy Joel

Perhaps because of retro-fifties moldy tomes that still hang around like *The Rules,* I get plentiful calls from women fearful about relationships. Even ones who are otherwise strong and capable still ask stuff like, "Did I say too much?" "Should I have been more coy?" or "Why didn't I play it cooler?"

But the forces of karma need no manipulation. After all these readings to all kinds of people, I know one thing for sure: If you're destined to be with someone, *nothing* can stop it. You won't need to rope, trick, or drug them into loving you. Those books that leave women terrified of just being themselves are somehow both tragic and hilarious at once.

A psychic teacher of mine used to say, "Karma is like a train. When it pulls up, it's almost impossible not to get on. And, for that matter, not to *stay* on until the last stop. For better or worse."

Well, here's my proof.

A guy named Eli called to say he had reunited with his ex, Elsa. Beside himself with delight, he wanted me to look at their charts for potential wedding dates. Suddenly, I remembered our initial reading the year before.

"Whoa, wait a minute!" I yelled, smacking my head with my hand. "Wasn't she the crazy chick who threw out all your clothes? You called me from your bathrobe, remember? You talked about getting a restraining order!"

Eli laughed as he reminded me that they had a huge blowout one night and he left the next morning for a business trip. While he was gone, Elsa, an Aries-artist-with-Leo-moon-total-Kali-incarnation if there ever was one, was still enraged.

So she took all his clothes, shoes, hats—even his precious vintage motorcycle jacket—and sold the whole lot at Crossroads Trading. (No Goodwill donations for *this* firecracker. She was gonna make some bucks off the deal to boot.)

Then she took the money and moved out.

He went to his IT job in sweats and flip-flops for a week until he could get new threads.

Yet now they were reunited and planning to wed.

"You know," he confessed, "she's a creative genius. And yes, she's a complete and total maniac. But she's *my* maniac. Did I tell you she has a new show opening next month on Potrero? I'll send you a mailing. Anyway, I'd be bored to death with anyone else."

He recently wrote to say the union remains "blissfully tempestuous."

And what more could you want if you choose to marry *Kali*?

That's how karma is. When something is right, prior lifetimes carve patterns of energetic familiarity and recognition. A template forged in the fires of the past clicks back in. People just fit.

Yiddish has a good word for this resonance, *bashert*. Meant to be.

So you can relax and be yourself.

If it's bashert, no need to behave "properly." You're not auditioning for a Broadway play.

And if it's not—well, you've probably just been saved a *whole* lot of trouble.

Say What You Mean

In a room where people unanimously
maintain a conspiracy of silence, one word
of truth sounds like a pistol shot.
—Czeslaw Milosz

Four ages, or yugas, cycle eternally through the Indian calendar. Right now we're in the final and most corrupt, the *Kali Yuga*, ruled by that much-maligned and misunderstood Goddess of Death and Transformation.

The scriptures said that in this time few people's words will match their actions. Or rather, people will lie. A lot.

To each other, and often, to *themselves*.

So it's supremely powerful in this time to make our word be good.

To do what we say and to say what we mean.

~~~

A charismatic guy named Greg called me once for a reading. He was committed to two different women in Denver

136

where he lived, and eager for each to think she was "the one."

"Listen," he told me, "I've got the *perfect* deal right now that I absolutely CANNOT blow."

One woman was intellectual and inspiring, the other was, well, just hot. He didn't want to risk losing either.

But the chaos and deception exhausted him completely. And after months of juggling, the two collided anyway.

Greg admitted, "Then *both* women eventually kicked my lyin' butt to the curb."

I explained how invoking Divine Order makes it so much easier to just tell the truth. He could say,

"The perfect partner is already picked. She'll arrive in the right time and the right way. Whoever is right is already selected and will come."

He didn't need to lie and manipulate from fear of loss. What was meant for him would happen.

Greg sent an email to say he'd been diligently calling this vibration into his personal life ever since we spoke. He was finally happily dating someone with the best qualities of *both* the women who had fled.

Mara, another client, told me her relationship has been over for years but insisted that she could never hurt her boyfriend with the truth. She was sure he could never handle it. But I told her that often it's just the *opposite*. By staying in a union she knows is over, she hobbles her partner from moving on. She actually *prevents* him from meeting someone who might be right.

Though many of us have done this, it's a strange kind of condescension.

So much better to pray for the courage to speak the truth with as much love, kindness, and clarity as possible. People are often eventually grateful to have acknowledgment of what deep in their hearts they actually already *know*.

When Odds Don't Matter

You don't have to know how to open the door yourself
but you might want to undo a deadbolt or two.

—Hiromi Min

Someone named Janine called wanting to know why she
hadn't been able to find the kind of union she'd been seeking forever. She'd finally decided that though she loved San
Francisco, she needed to move to a spot with better "odds."
Every potential guy here, she moaned, was either married,
gay, or both. I passionately assured her this wasn't so, saying, "It's not about *numbers*, it's about karma and vibration. And you don't need a hundred options. Unless you're
secretly a Mormon, you only need *one*."

But her mind was set. She was moving to the Ultimate
He-Man Valhalla: Alaska.

I was flummoxed. "Do you actually *want* to live there?"

"Silly," she replied. "Absolutely not. I belong here. But
the ratio of women to guys is like eighty-five to one. I *must*
go."

I said she might spare herself a pricey and exhausting move just by using Divine Order. So she agreed for the next month to say, *"The perfect partner is already selected. He is arriving in the right way at the right time. I am so grateful to receive him."*

But she wanted to cover all her bases and continued to pack for the tundra.

I kept insisting that if she sincerely invoked Divine Order, a relationship would come at the right time. She didn't have to hunt. She could draw the experience by feeling worthy to receive and following the leads that appeared. But she had to feel *deserving*. She didn't need to move somewhere she dreaded. I even told her about my friend Ana who lived like a cloistered nun but ended up falling madly in love with the visiting cable repair girl.

But Janine was undeterred.

By the end of the summer she left, calling me from the airport for a tearful good-bye.

By Halloween the phone rang. Janine in Juneau.

"Hey, are you ready?" she teased. "Oh, jeez, you already *know* what I'm gonna say. I got here and honestly it was so completely ridiculous. Gorgeous place but I so didn't belong. But I kept doing that Divine Order deal since what the hell, I'd already come.

"Then one night this guy started talking to me in a café who was on vacation, visiting . . ."

I interrupted, ". . . from *here*?"

"Ooh, yeh, mama. You got it," she laughed. "Twelve blocks from my flat in the Mission. The *most* amazing person. We've spent the last month running around Alaska together in total heaven. He jokes that maybe we needed to start off first with a pricey vacation. I'm moving back tomorrow."

Giving the World a Heart

When it's over I want to say, I was the bride
married to amazement; I was the bridegroom
taking the whole world in my arms.
—Mary Oliver

I've had an ambivalent relationship to Valentine's Day since I was a teen. Odd because with Libra Rising and being born the Year of the Sheep, I've got a romantic streak as deep as the Caspian Sea. But it's always just seemed *wrong* that a holiday of the heart would have such narrow parameters and limited goals. As if the strongest force on the planet could only have been created for one other special person to receive.

The Universal Shakti just seems so much more diverse and innovative than that.

Maybe it's my four planets in Aquarius, but I often think of love in a global, not just personal, way. Wouldn't it be great if there was a day where *everyone* blanketed this tired, ailing planet with an unbridled, riotous array of bless-

142

ings? With random acts of kindness and senseless acts of beauty like that old saying?

~~~

One particular Valentine's Day years ago changed my life. A brilliant butch playwright-goddess-girl who rode a black Kawasaki ended our union—on February 12. I stood in a phone booth on Valencia Street sobbing to a friend.

From the corner of my eye I saw a homeless guy walk by pushing a shopping cart, glancing my way. A few minutes later he returned.

"For you, lady," he said, looking straight into me and offering a perfect huge white gardenia that I had no blessed idea where he could have possibly found. "Don't cry, baby, it'll all work out. I promise."

So of course, I cried harder. And gave him a big hug and every bill in my purse. Something about him just cracked my heart open to fill the sky.

The next day, rather than whining about the surprise breakup, I felt inspired by this guy. I moved around the city just anonymously helping. I saw how many people, in relationships or not, felt profoundly miserable on this Alleged Big Day of Love. It felt incredible just to give to whoever crossed my path.

I held a prayer all day: *Wherever I can be a force for Love, please guide me. Take me wherever you wish me to go. Let me do your bidding.*

Surefire route to The. Best. Valentine's. Day. Ever.

Or maybe Best. Life. Ever.

Whether you've got a terrific partner,

or *not*.

Chapter Twelve

MUNDANE MIRACLES AND OTHER MYSTERIES

The $700 Penthouse

> God will make a way out of no way.
> —Anonymous

I'm a great believer in what some traditions would call *conjuring a miracle*, inviting Divine intercession on just about any topic, big or small. People often tell me about situations so overwhelming and complex, their rational minds cannot begin to fathom a way out. Sometimes they're surrounded by friends and family who might even ratchet up their sense of powerlessness and despair. But over the years I've seen that calling in a miracle can open doors that linear rationality never could.

I mentioned earlier that I once spent three years in bed

145

with a rare failure of my endocrine system. Eventually a gifted acupuncturist arrived who restored my health in nine months.

But that wasn't the only miracle.

Once my health began returning, I needed a new apartment. While I was bedridden, I honestly didn't care that I lived in a small, dark room with a mat on the floor and a hot plate. As I started to feel like a semifunctional human again, I longed for a real home.

I had barely been able to work for years and had almost no funds. However, my mind, pliant and awestruck from my recent healing, was wide, wide open to being surprised.

How great that almost no one was around to tell me how "unrealistic" this was. Or to remind me of the astronomical San Francisco housing market. I was wholeheartedly and fully receptive to a miracle. Jeez, I had just returned from the dead. I had *nothing* to lose.

One day I was on a short walk in my Richmond neighborhood. Three blocks from my cave on Geary, I saw a sign: *Penthouse for Rent*. A tall, swarthy, genial-looking guy stood nearby. "Want to come up and see?" he asked, grinning.

"Well, I can't imagine how I could ever afford such a place," I laughed ruefully, "but why *not*? You never know."

"Yes," he agreed, beaming, "That's the one damn thing for sure in this life. You just *never* know."

We went upstairs and the place was astonishing. Not

large but with floor-to-ceiling views of the Golden Gate Bridge, vaulted skylights, hardwood floors, vibrant energy.

"I don't even dare ask what this costs," I sighed.

"Well, what are you paying right now?" he asked.

And here's what happened. While the apartment was supposed to be rented for a couple thousand a month, this angel gave it to me for just two hundred more than my hovel.

He said, "I'm from Syria. I grew up in the Damascus streets and learned by the age of four to read someone's character on the *spot*. It's a matter of life and death, you know? The minute you walked up I knew three things: I could trust you, you'd been through a disaster, and I wanted you to live here. You were perfect."

So that's how Divine Order brought my San Francisco penthouse for the next three years, the absolute right stretch of time. Eventually the building converted to condos and I passed it on to a friend who bought it.

Sometimes reality is terribly unrealistic.

Que Sera Sera: The Errant Bullet

Let life happen to you. Life is in the right, always.
— Rainer Maria Rilke

The day after Thanksgiving I gave a reading to Corrine, who's almost a real-life Lara Croft, Tomb Raider. A Gemini with a Sag Moon, she's an expert in hang gliding and windsurfing, teaches mountaineering and scuba diving, and has ridden her Harley across half of Asia.

Alone.

I used to think I was pretty adventurous, but compared to Corrine, I'm just one quivering mass of Capricorn cowardice.

In thirty years of full-on adventure she'd never had more than a few scraped knees and some food poisoning. Nonetheless, she called because in the early dawn of Thanksgiving she stepped out of bed and tripped on the rawhide chewing bone of her miniature collie.

And broke her foot.

Overwhelmed by irony, she had to cancel her upcoming climb in Nepal.

She was also aware that she hadn't been "stopped" in thirty years. For months she'd been trying to write a manuscript about her travels but couldn't make time.

Here was her chance.

Stuff like this makes me feel at times like an optimistic fatalist. Some things happen just because they're simply *meant* to happen. All the precautions in the world won't stop them. Yet viewed through a positive lens, even those fated events may eventually be seen as lucky.

Before I moved to San Francisco's quiet Outer Richmond in the late eighties, I'd spent several years in the heart of the Mission. I loved the pulse of the place back then, the great music, Mexican food, and general joie de vivre. I was in heaven, living on burritos, dance classes, and yoga in Dolores Park.

Then I got sick, and my rational cautious self thought I should move to a "safer" neighborhood. The Mission was a major crime hub back then. Though I'd never felt any personal danger, I thought I might heal better in the burbs.

Little did I know.

One day, drinking tea in my peaceful penthouse, I heard a loud whiz followed by the breaking of glass and a crash.

A bullet had struck the window right above my head, then pierced the wall behind me, zipping through the kitchen and into the bath.

I found it lodged in a shattered shower tile.

Until the police arrived I sat on the cold bathroom floor staring mutely at the wall, my heart pounding through my ribs like a drum, trying to figure out what the hell had just occurred.

The cops told me a rare gang shoot-out had happened two blocks away. Somehow a stray bullet from a high-powered rifle landed in my top-floor hideaway in San Francisco's statistically safest neighborhood.

"Jeez, I thought I'd seen *everything*," one of the officers said, shaking her head. "Do you realize if you had stood up a moment earlier you'd be dead now?"

I wanted to make the bullet into a necklace but she smiled and took it away.

As evidence.

Two from the God Annals

You may wear out your iron-soled shoes searching for
what arrives without effort when the time is right.
—Chinese proverb

The world isn't made up of atoms.
It's made up of stories.
—Muriel Rukeyser

My former neighbor Amy desperately needed a new vehicle. She and her husband, Todd, were in a grueling winter in upstate New York and their Trooper was dying. They couldn't find the right car yet resisted spending money to fix the old. Months passed as they looked everywhere, becoming completely exhausted. Finally they invoked Divine Order, affirming that the perfect vehicle would come at the right time, and reluctantly spent fifteen hundred dollars to fix their clunker.

A week later a woman pulled up at a stoplight in an unusual green Forester, their instant dream car. Finding out where she bought it, they drove to her distant dealership that afternoon. A mile before the shop they started giggling as they entered Endwell, New York. A moment later they saw the store sitting on the corner of Amy Road. "I mean, really," said Todd, shaking his head. "Who could make this junk up?"

Only later did they see they weren't able to find the right new car until they had surrendered and fixed the old one. In the end they needed both.

Now here's what happened when I was Amy's neighbor twenty years back.

We lived side by side on a bucolic country road in the Catskills during an awful time when challenges circled me like a flock of ravens. I loved to sit on my little porch and contemplate my misery. (The idea of Divine Order hadn't exactly taken firm hold yet. Believe me, it's a process.) Sometimes as I sat brooding, I imagined buying latticework to grow ivy and purple bougainvillea. Just the image would lift my heart. But I told Amy sadly that even driving fifty miles to the nearest lumber shop was overwhelming.

I did periodically remember to ask God for help. Every so often I would halfheartedly mumble to the Force that I couldn't really feel but needed to pretend existed, "Okay, I'm totally lost. Any sign I'm not alone will do right now. *Please?*"

One day a big truck came barreling along, unheard of

on our quiet road. A moment later, I saw Amy slapping her thighs, howling with laughter.

"Oh, my God! You won't *believe* what just fell off that thing!" she yelled as the truck vanished around the corner.

A huge piece of lattice the exact size I needed had been dropped and delivered by the side of the road.

Celestial Clockwork

Be grateful for the karma you don't have.

—Anonymous

The other day I was driving home when I hit what in my small town was an unusual, major traffic jam. The Park Street bridge had opened to let through a large ship at the same time the last of rush hour hit. A line of cars dragged for blocks with no escape route. I watched the people around me grow more agitated by the minute.

I decided to just let go, take a deep breath, and inwardly say, "My *life is unfolding in Divine timing. All delays are beneficial. I'm always at the right place at the right time*." Growing up as a really impatient child (you know, Mars conjunct Saturn in Sagittarius), this statement has really altered my life.

So I turned up some Lady Gaga, wrote in my journal, and chilled. In about twenty minutes I was on my way.

When I got home I saw the blessing. Four squad cars

154

and two ambulances packed my street. Twenty minutes ear-lier a drunk driver had skidded out of control in front of my building, bashing like a pinball into seven different vehicles, one by one. Without the delay I might have been right in the line of fire.

My friend Tom told me a similar story that happened to him in reverse. He had taken his beloved boyfriend home to meet his family in Buffalo for the first time. All had gone reasonably well. Even his rather fundamentalist father was uncommonly gracious and kind.

But the night before their scheduled departure, the dad suddenly went mad. He decided the "sinners" could not be in his home a moment longer. They had to go. While his loving mom stood by apologizing and crying, Tom and his partner threw their luggage in the car in a frenzy, speeding out of town like a band on the run. "It was," he reminisced tartly, "quite the exciting little psychodrama."

They decided to drive all night to get back to the en-lightened world of Manhattan.

Later that evening they saw the cosmic handiwork. A freak blizzard had gathered from nowhere, hitting Buffalo two days early. The news showed cars abandoned by the side of the New York Thruway like empty carcasses buried under three feet of snow. The National Guard was called out, emergency shelters were set up.

"If my dad hadn't gone stark raving ballistic, we would

have been trapped. The storm front was precisely where we would have been driving. The Universe expelled us at the perfect time."

You just never know what blessings an obstacle or problem may be creating, and what larger nightmares you might totally be spared.

Chapter Thirteen

CONTESTANTS MUST BE PRESENT TO WIN

When Travel Isn't Enough

Be here now. Be somewhere else later. Is that so hard?
—Jewish-Zen saying

When I was growing up in Pennsylvania I had a small framed photo in my bedroom of a woman's hand gripping a suitcase. The caption said, "She was often seized with a desire to be somewhere else."

For years I was consumed with a wanderlust that is perhaps endemic with three planets in Sagittarius. And the truth is, I'm *never* more at home than when I'm traveling. I used to fantasize about exotic plane tickets and a passport filled with colorful visas the way some people long to have children or a Porsche.

Yet along the way something happened. I noticed that often a trip I organized would be preemptively blocked. Once a partner and I booked a three-month journey to India, Bali, and Thailand that I'd constructed in my mind for years, like someone might obsessively craft a perfect house. Right before we bought the tickets, so many ludicrously intense obstructions arose we could only laugh— and cancel.

I once had a talented astrologer tell me that I'd spent countless incarnations roaming the earth like a vagabond. But she said, "Hey, you've already *seen* it all before. How many lifetimes can you keep running?" This time, she said, I was going inward, learning to surrender to life *as* it was, right *where* I was. Learning to be still, to bless and embrace it all, without limitation, without escape.

I knew she was right.

~~~

I remember sitting in a sushi bar in the Mission. You never know who will bring you to a crossroads. While I ate my maki roll, a woman started to talk to a guy at another table visiting from Denmark. She began a loud travelogue.

"Oh, yes," she said, "we did northern Italy last fall. Oh, a must, must-do. And before that we bagged Belgium and Prague and Berlin and oh, of course, Provence, and Paris.

Well, you know, darling, we *always* do Paris." She poked the air with her chopstick for emphasis. "I mean, how can you not? That's not even an *option*, is it? You might as well *die*." Wrinkling her nose at the very thought, she continued, "and then Helsinki and Stockholm, well, they always improve, don't they? A good solid B-plus I'd say . . . and oh, my dear, the tapas in Barcelona . . ."

As the young Dane tried to politely listen, his eyes glazing over, the woman went on.

And on.

And on.

~~~

The longer I listened, the more tired I became, a kind of profound bottomless existential exhaustion. I felt I might drown right there in We-Be Sushi, face down in my miso soup, from the sheer futility of it all. This woman's relentless chase of the world's mirages left me utterly, thoroughly spent.

I mentally thanked her as I got up to leave.

I paid my bill and stepped into the music of Valencia Street, giddy with nowhere to go and nothing to see.

Some mariachi players carried their guitars into La Rondalla, laughing and joking in Spanish.

Two cute blond boys sat in a café, holding hands, drinking espresso.

A woman with spiky purple hair walked by in a red halter on her way to yoga, her mat in one arm, miniature poodle in the other.

Her whole back was tattooed with the jagged-edged open wings of a great blue heron, ready to fly.

Zen of Traffic

*Mastering others is strength; mastering
yourself is true power.*

—Lao Tzu

The other day my client Tina complained that events were preventing her from going on a spiritual retreat she'd planned for months. After sympathizing for a half hour I finally said, "You know, maybe you don't even *need* one right now. After all, the Universe is blocking it.

"And look," I said, waving her cards, "here's the Chariot and eight of Wands. It's about your *vehicle*. Why not just be conscious when you drive? You know, everything you need spiritually you could learn right in your car."

She said I was completely bananas.

"Maybe," I giggled. "But then why on earth do you call?"

Yet I really wasn't joking. The Zen of driving can develop all kinds of virtues:

Trusting there's enough. When a person dives in like a raven and takes someone's parking space, I often figure she doesn't trust there's another spot with her own name on it. But really, if you're moving with the flow, you don't have to worry. When someone nabs your spot you can think, "Good, they *need* it. And I always find what I need, too." Another space invariably comes.

Generosity. Some people maneuver like everyone else is an obstacle. But driving is an easy place to be kind. There's always time to let other people merge into a lane, or even go ahead of you. And often they'll pay it forward to the next car.

Being with what is. Sometimes there's nothing to do but surrender. But if you pray to let go and enjoy the ride, something happens. Usually fighting reality is worse than the traffic itself.

Abundance. My friend Cynthia taught me this. I used to park blocks away from a destination as soon as I saw something. She would scold me, laughing, "No, no, no! At least drive by *first* to see if the perfect space is waiting. Why do you assume it's *not*?"

Compassion. I love to be in the car when my pal Chi from Alabama drives. Once when someone cut her off and flipped her the bird, she drawled, "Why that poor child just didn't get enough lovin' when he was little! Betcha he never even got breast-fed as a baby. That's why people do all this junk later, you know."

And she really meant it.

Equanimity. Being able to breathe and be calm behind the wheel is a huge achievement. Someone might be able to hold a tripod headstand for an hour while chanting two hundred Sanskrit verses and tossing a salad with her toes but still be defeated—by her car.

Zen of Traffic Postscript: Dude, Where's My Car?

Just think how lucky you are today
to only have this much karma.

—Anonymous

August 20, 2009, New Moon in Leo.

10:44 a.m. I post a column at examiner.com called *The Zen of Traffic*. Try to make a few salient points along the way.

2:45 p.m. Drive to Rainbow, the resplendent San Francisco collective grocery store, to shop.

2:55 p.m. Park Prius in a commercial zone outside the store that has signs saying *No parking till 3:00 p.m.* Figure with only five minutes to go I'm totally safe.

3:02 p.m. Hear Rainbow worker announce over loud-speaker that someone's blue Prius is being towed. Run outside to see my car being dragged down Folsom. I'm in shock trying to figure out how the hell a truck could even arrive and chain me up so fast.

3:30 p.m. Sprint the twelve blocks to the tow yard at Seventh and Bryant to join a line of folks who all had their cars taken in the same "sting." The clerk confides the city's strategies had recently changed. San Francisco is broke and desperate for revenue. So while you used to be able to park five or ten minutes early, now a traffic cop and tow truck lie in wait at certain spots ready to pounce.

4:15 p.m. Pay $373 (not including the $125 ticket arriving in mail) to reclaim hijacked Prius.

4:45 p.m. Drive back to finish shopping at Rainbow. Discover the cart I had put aside filled with food at customer service has been emptied and used by someone else. Refill cart with each object, feeling eerily like Bill Murray in *Groundhog Day.*

And yet, a part of me is cracking up.

I mean, I'd definitely have preferred to spend that money differently. But you gotta love it. What a test to see if I could even remotely live what I wrote.

Anyway, today was a NEW MOON at twenty-seven degrees Leo, on top of my Pluto and Jupiter, opposing my Moon and Venus, and squaring Mars and Saturn.

Something *had* to happen.

And you never know what I might have missed. Maybe instead of a serious accident, I got away easy with an exorbitant surprise towing.

You never know.

Contestants Must Be Present to Win

If you were in your body you'd be home by now.
—Berkeley bumper sticker

One day I became seriously motivated to become more present. I was driving onto the Bay Bridge one afternoon, lost in thought. The next thing I knew the toll-taker was yanking me out of my reverie, saying sharply, "Honey, what in Lord's name do you want me to do with this sorry thang? It sure ain't gonna get you across no damn bridge!"

I realized I had handed her my garage-door opener. While I chuckled about it for an hour, I knew had a problem.

So now I stop often during the day to ask, "Where am I? What am I doing right this minute? Where has my mind taken me?"

And most of all, "Am I breathing?"

It also has helped to simply plug into the earth each morning like a healthy, strong tree. I imagine having a long tap root that goes all the way into the earth's center, unshakable despite outer turbulence. When I'm about to drive, I even root through the floor of the car to keep me attentive.

Nonetheless, being more grounded is a real work in progress. Certainly some of us, especially many creative sorts, can get easily lost in "alternate" realities. And spiritual communities, even yoga classes, can sometimes be filled with folks longing to avoid the grit of the present for the buzzing high of bliss.

But what if it's all the same? A false dichotomy. God really *is* in the details. All the messy, earthly details.

～～

I once lived in an apartment building where one of my neighbors was an otherworldly, charismatic woman from a local temple. She had a wonderful singing voice and often invited everyone over to chant or meditate. She'd had many spiritual teachers around the world and flamboyant inner visions that she loved to share. Most people in the building found her utterly endearing and completely maddening.

You see, she seemed to treat reality as a pesky distraction from her spiritual seeking. What good were all those celestial visions if she moved people's still-wet clothes when she needed the dryer? How did chanting help if she left her trash everywhere for some kind of cosmic pickup? Often she would wander away as someone spoke.

On the night she moved out, she somehow entangled her U-Haul in the row of bulbs that lit our garage. As she hightailed from the building for the final time, she pulled the whole electrical strip off the wall and then dragged it behind her down the road, loudly clattering all the way. My neighbors and I watched in bemused wonder as our cars were plunged into darkness. The damage took weeks to be repaired.

A couple of us later remembered that her adopted name in Sanskrit meant "Bearer of Divine Light."

Hit the Road with God

And I will show you a third way, a hidden way.
—Anonymous

I've become a rabid fan of Divine Order for one good reason. For all my supposed intelligence, I would routinely feel overwhelmed and frozen by life's never-ending problems and decisions.

Nowadays I feel lucky that my personality's own limitations forced me to become dependent on the help of the cosmos. Perhaps if I had been born an efficient superwoman I wouldn't have needed *any* of this. But learning to move with the Divine flow changed my reality completely. It turned what was once a road of total stress and fatigue to one of comparative ease, or at least manageability.

For example, whenever I travel I invoke Divine Order to open the way. It's like having a cosmic advance team. Ahead of departure, I imagine the whole trip surrounded by light and energy, saying:

Let every aspect of this journey unfold in harmony. Let Divine Order arrange and show me every detail. The right airline connections, lodging, and all else are already selected and I'll be guided to them easily. I'll follow the leads as they are shown.

I've used this to help create seats on previously sold-out planes, find cheap rental cars, whisk through clogged security lines, and have an often fun, relaxed time under absolutely nutty conditions.

Not every door opens like magic (though they sometimes do), but the way is eased or at least made tolerable. Maybe think of it like WD-40 on the etheric plane. Rather than depending on the push of the ego, you travel with abundant help. You feel as if you're in a holy chariot being carried to your destination. You're shown the right openings at the right time. *And you can relax into what you're powerless to change until an alternate route is shown.*

~~~

Before GPS systems and iPhones were ubiquitous, I was visiting Los Angeles when a gunman shut down all lanes on Highway 5. There I was, trapped outside Glendale, thirty-five miles from my destination, in a mass of cars solid as a glacier. After an hour, people were going pretty cuckoo. The beefy bald guy in the next truck started smashing his roof with something that looked like an anvil. I felt like I was in the sequel to *Blade Runner*.

I called in Divine Order and spent another hour crawling to an exit. Pulling into a gas station, I continued to pray.

Then a preternaturally cheerful young woman at the next pump and I started to chat. It turned out she, too, was heading for Long Beach. And she told me proudly that as a native she knew how to do it all off-freeway, with shortcuts, too.

I followed the Devi with the auburn ponytail in her seagreen RX-7 through a hundred twists and turns for the next two hours. She even waved me over once at a great taqueria.

A half mile from my hotel she flashed her lights good-bye.

I silently thanked her with my whole heart for being the consummate guide.

Chapter Fourteen

THE HIGHER OCTAVE

Be Your Whole Dazzling Chart

Follow the grain in your own wood.
—Howard Thurman

While I was eating at a café in Ojai, California, a guy wearing a poncho and a straw hat walked up to say he had an important message from my angels. Ojai being Ojai (a vortex for all things new age, groovy, or sometimes insane), this seemed like the most natural thing in the world.

So I invited him to sit down.

His message was brief. He closed his eyes and spoke as if he was transmitting from a staccato radio, "You. Unusual. Half and half. Everything. Introvert, extrovert. East, West. Brain, heart. Young, old. Woman, man. Everything. No forget."

173

Then he left to go buy a burrito.

Well, this was so accurate he didn't know the half of it. I'd spent years trying to dissolve the innate paradoxes of my nature until I realized one day we were born to *embrace* them. My planets in Aquarius and Sag were the life of the party, but a strong Neptune longed to hide at home. The Capricorn Sun worked like a dog, but my Libra Rising only wanted a hot tub. On and on.

I had to learn how to let all the different conflicting parts speak with abandon. Those online tests where you're deemed a "type" were impossible. Depending on my mood or time of day, the answers would shift just like my illegible handwriting.

So I tend to attract clients ablaze with contradictions like Lee, the vivacious Sag from Los Angeles. She has a ton of fire, yet until recently her Scorp Moon ran the show. It filled her life with a steady diet of emotional Sturm und Drang while her poor fire signs suffocated, longing for fun and adventure. But now she's owning her Sag and aging in reverse, becoming the spontaneous spirit she repressed in her younger days.

Someone else called me recently from Germany. She had a batch of planets in grounded Taurus, yet her Aries Moon sat next to rebel Uranus. When I suggested she might be living a more cautious life than her unconventional Moon pined for, she whooped loudly and vigorously agreed.

A dutiful Virgo I know with practical Saturn on his Sun

graduated from law school to appease his father. But within six months of practicing, he had ulcers. His array of planets in Libra cried for art and beauty, so eventually he opened a boutique in New York. He confessed, "Honey, I was without a doubt the world's *worst* attorney. I'd be in the middle of a deposition dreaming of giving everyone a makeover. I'd never been around people with *less* style. It was like working in a special rung of Brooks Brothers hell."

Sometimes I think the different planets in someone's chart are like guests at a cosmic party.

Some aspects blend, others clash.

The trick is helping everyone feel included and comfortable.

Just make sure no one takes over and drinks all the punch.

Are You Plutonic?

A person is truly free, even here in this embodied
state, if he knows that God is the true agent
and he himself is powerless to do anything.
                                    —Ramakrishna

She's got Bette Davis eyes.

                                    —Kim Carnes

When I was nineteen, I was lucky to be taken to an astrologer who knocked my socks off. I arrived at her home filled with confusion and self-doubt, and left with a map of my potential. It was my first experience of being seen.

When she saw my chart had many tight angles, especially to Saturn and Pluto, I remember her saying this was a "short-leash" incarnation.

"Your horoscope has fast turnaround," she explained, running her hand through her short gray hair and gazing at me with kind eyes. "Some people delay the consequences of their actions for another life; they need a rest. But your kickback is immediate, for better or worse. Don't forget you wanted it that way." She laughed drily, "You're on the karmic pay-as-you-go plan."

I was actually filled with relief. Until then I didn't know why such crazy things were always happening. Like the time I slightly swiped this polished black BMW that was parked by my dorm. "Oh, the owner is so wealthy, it doesn't matter," I thought.

The next morning my window had been smashed and the stereo stolen.

That sort of stuff.

~~

So, how do you know if you're Plutonic?

Well, if you could relate to that story.

Or if you're Scorpio Sun, Moon, or Ascendant, since Pluto rules that. Or if you have Pluto making strong angles to any of those points or others. Or if you have a bunch of planets all in the House of Scorpio, number eight.

So you could be a Pisces or Gemini who acts like a Scorp simply because Pluto sits on your horizon or squares your Sun.

Even if you don't know a scrap of astrology, you're likely this type if you've been asked forever, "Why are you so intense?" "Must you be obsessed?" or "Are you *always* a maniac?"

Luckily Plutonic sorts usually find each other in their dogged search for depth and transformation. (Good thing, because others may find them a bit, well, unnerving.)

You also may be Plutonic if you don't evoke neutrality. People tend to either love or hate you.

Or if you have X-ray eyes that look to the bottom of . . . anything.

Or if you're a sensation-freak of sorts. Being ruled by the planet of death and rebirth, the goddesses Kali and Durga, Pluto people often seek transcendence spiritually, sexually, intellectually, creatively, or any damn or blessed way imaginable.

On the low road, they can get embroiled in power struggles, manipulations, and resentments galore. But when that route is abandoned, higher options emerge.

At the highest this drive can bring spiritual enlightenment, awakening to one's true nature, burning away any attachment to the small self. Pluto can help one fly free from the cage of ego.

So can you relate?

Are you Plutonic?

You'll definitely know.

The Higher Octave

If you don't know it, you can't blow it.
—Louis Armstrong

I am available for anything that wants
to happen in this moment, including
that which is beyond imagining.
—P. Lowe

The other day a teenage friend was saying how all her current problems came from her sign.

"You're an astrologer," she said. "So you know how all Scorpios are envious, right? We're controlling, vindictive, ruthless. That's just how it goes. We want what we want."

"Good god, girl," I said, laughing and throwing my arm around her shoulder. "What bad astrology books have YOU been reading? You're just describing the *worst* of your sign. Like a Pluto remainder item you'd get in the dollar bin at Walmart. There are higher octaves, you know."

Scorpio in fact has three forms, with the lowest being

the stinging *Scorpion* she described. But as the sign evolves and purifies, the energy of the *Eagle* emerges, bestowing clarity, vision, and courage.

And eventually the *Phoenix*, the magical bird with the power of rebirth, arises from the ashes. No Phoenix wastes her time on resentments and revenge when she can be joyously, exuberantly soaring to the sun.

In a given lifetime, the vast reservoirs of power all Scorpios have can be used to reach one of these more elevated expressions, or can be wasted on retribution and vendettas.

But *every* sign has a high and low frequency. And *nothing* in a chart is inherently bad. Every one has potential luminosity and grace.

In fact, my own has sixteen squares, which in classical astrology would have been called "afflicted beyond belief." But a reader told me early on, "Use your potential wisely. All those squares give a ton of energy. You'll either be really helpful to people. Or a little nuts."

Or both.

In a way, we're each here to express the music of our soul. So if yours sounds like jazz, then *be* jazz. If it's shakuhachi flute, be that. If Black Sabbath, then what the hell, how'd you find this book anyway? Sometimes I think we're drawn to the music in a given lifetime that we literally *are*, that carries our unique nature.

Astrology gives a miraculous lens into each individual's

Divine perfection. Then the culture's silly fixation on competition and comparison falls away. No need to compare yourself to anyone.

In fact, you might just shudder at the thought.

Your own karma is plenty.

The Cosmic Orchestra

If you call forth what is in you, it will save you. If you
do not call forth what is in you, it will destroy you.
—Gospel of Saint Thomas

No one can give you what you don't
feel willing to receive yourself.
—Anonymous

Astrology shows each soul's special gifts and beauty. But no one is just their Sun sign. Since the Moon and Rising signs are as important as the Sun, most of us are a complex melange.

That's why when you pick up a generalized astrology book giving characteristics for your "sign," it may not fit at all. I may be a Capricorn, but having Moon, Mercury, and Venus in iconoclastic Aquarius, I sure don't behave much like one. Whenever I read the descriptions of staid, gloomy, ambitious Capricorns I just laugh. On the other hand, my friend Ed fits the Saturnian stereotype well but doesn't have other conflicting signs.

I love, too, how charts operate outside of gender. We still get all kinds of cultural nonsense about how men and women *should* be. But astrology doesn't give one hoot. Everyone has a mix of masculinity and femininity depending on their chart, not their gender or even their sexuality.

My younger brother is a Cancer born the Chinese Boar year with a strong domestic streak. To his wife's delight, the guy adores cooking, cleaning, and raising his brood when he's not at work. I can scarcely imagine how that might feel.

~~~

I spoke with Teresa, a frequent client who's a true warrior-queen. She was born with Mars sitting smack on her Aries horizon, along with an Aries Moon: pure, undiluted yang power. She's been accused repeatedly of "false advertising" when dates discover the steel hidden beneath her curves and mascara. She fruitlessly tried to follow simplistic advice books like *Men Are from Mars* that told her to be soft and girly.

But I said, "Look, *every* chart has a fit. Go date someone who is *seeking* a tigress. Believe me, he's absolutely out there. I promise."

Finally she decided to stop suppressing her nature.

I was so relieved. I mean, would a tiger of *any* gender try to behave like a bunny?

Now she's with a Taurus who has a ton of Aries himself. He told her meeting a match as brilliant and strong as Teresa was like winning the lottery.

She owned the force of her chart and immediately drew someone who was supremely grateful.

Chapter Fifteen

BE WHO YOU
ARE, REALLY

Why Bother Competing?

> *We're all winners you know.*
> —Crystal Bowersox

> *I never wanted to be the best. I just
> wanted to be the best damn me.*
> —Lily Tomlin

Weird. Maybe it's the Mercury Retrograde. My inbox was
filled all week with three different people pestering me to
help their friends become "Spiritual Author of the Year" in
some insane online contest.

I wrote back to say there were so many things wrong
with this idea, I barely knew where to begin.

I mean, a spiritual book *contest*? Like those world yoga

trials where people cram to do the most handstands or alternate nostril breaths in an hour?

Talk about oxymorons.

I remember one New Year's Day my pals at Monkey Yoga in Oakland held an event. Whoever did the longest backbend got a stuffed monkey or a used, ragged towel or something. But that was a *joke*.

So when I got these emails I thought, okay, I know we live in a culture where scarcity and competition are enshrined to the core. But wouldn't a bona fide *spiritual book* aspire a little higher than this?

I mean, why be locked in the same old dog-eat-dog paradigm that's brought the world to the brink of extinction?

And why even have a *best*? Would you really need a smackdown between the *Bhagavad Gita* and the Bible? Or between the *Ramayana* and the Koran?

Buy your tickets here.

After all, this view of life as one brawling fight with winners and losers is awfully confining. With God as your Source, no one's good can *ever* take your own. With some focused attention, you can tap into the Divine flow at any point; what's meant to happen will eventually come. And if you write a book from a particular and pure vibration, everyone who needs to find it *will*, one way or another. No need to compete.

And anyway, can't one person's success actually bolster another's?

Why the heck not?

Rejecting Rejection

There is no rejection. Your charts either fit
or they don't. Karma or no karma.
          —Marlene, my first astrology teacher

Care about people's approval and
you become their prisoner.

                              —Lao Tzu

I consider each astrology chart like a piece of music. Anyone you mesh well with has a complementary vibe. A har-
monious song is thrumming in each of your souls.

Once you know that, you never have to believe in rejection again. No one can reject or "dump" you. The people
who match you, one way or another, will come. The ones
who don't will fall away.

I think my own chart sits on the crazy Uranian corner
where the funkiest of funk hooks up with Mozart, rock and
roll, and some hip-hop Hindu *bhajans*. People who love
paradox and contradiction often find me—others just run.

I heard from a friend who had just started teaching at

USF. Diane had just received her first evaluations and was shaken. While forty comments were glowing, one review cut so deeply she vowed to never teach again. The guy said her class had probably been "the single biggest waste of time he'd known this entire incarnation."

"Wow," I laughed, "you gotta admire his sense of drama. *You* were worse than all of junior high school? Worse than watching the Clinton impeachment trials? Worse than *Spider-Man 3*?

"And anyway, maybe the class really *was* a waste for him? Maybe nothing could have made that poor dude happy. And what if his chart had twenty squares with yours? He might have walked into the room and hated you on sight. That happens.

"Besides," I continued, "if everyone loves you, you're probably playing *waaay* too safe. If you're real, at least a few people might be annoyed. A little criticism sometimes can be an awfully *good* sign."

A Ma'am Is Not What I Am

> *Baby, I was born this way.*
> —Lady Gaga

> *I'm not going to die because I failed as someone*
> *else. I'd rather just succeed at being me.*
> —Margaret Cho

The other day I was cruising down Haight Street when I got stopped by a twentyish guy with long blond dreads rustling up donations for Greenpeace.

"Ma'am . . ." he ventured, "want to help the whales?" I shot him a stern "no" and kept going.

Then I felt bad and decided to go back.

"Listen," I said, as warmly as I could. "If you wanna get more money, maybe use a different greeting? No woman in this neighborhood will give you a dime once you call us THAT."

"Wow," he said, intrigued. "No offense meant. But it's true. Only the guys are giving to me." Then he grinned,

"And I did have a lady say she'd take my nuts off next time I said that."

"What?" I laughed. "And you *still* are?"

"Well, I don't know any other word for 'older' women. Do you?"

"You know, an all-purpose 'miss' would do. Even 'hey you' can be quite nice." Then I smiled and handed him some bills.

~~~

You know, I've been puzzling over this ma'am thing for a while. I don't aspire to look young, because that would be silly; I just look like *me*. I'm way past forty, yet I've always had a certain personal aesthetic: a little rock and roll, some punk, a bit of Asian-influenced femmy queer glamour. I don't see that changing. And with four planets in Aquarius, I'm as much the bohemian, artsy type now as I was thirty years ago when I first fled out West.

I've got spiky hennaed hair and usually live in skinny jeans, T-shirts, and silver jewelry. A strong yoga practice has (some of) me in better shape than when I smoked Camel nonfilters and downed margaritas as a spiritual practice at age twenty-five.

So how can I relate to "ma'am"?

The world is awash with women like me, straight, gay, bi, all sorts. Every one I know detests this priggish term.

Maybe it's the insanity that says women expire like bottles of milk.

Or maybe it's the sheer sexism of the language. Men have "sir" covering *everyone* while with women, it's age-based. "Miss" applies until some vague crossroads when you're pitched into the etymological junkyard of "ma'am."

Oddly, I don't mind the different titles for older and younger women when I leave the States. In India, I found *madame* elegant and charming. In French it sounds like a sensual verbal massage. I can even happily roll in Mexico with a *señora* or two.

So what is it with "ma'am"? Is it just because it sounds like spam, or damn, or mammogram? Visions of dentures and large-print *Reader's Digest*s waltz in my head.

Or is it because I grew up worshipping Tina Turner and Chrissie Hynde? I mean, could *they* ever be ma'ams? Could Joan Jett? Ellen? Amy Tan?

Yet the culture still pins this word on women like a wilted corsage.

But you know, the ultimate spiritual attainment might be when ma'am doesn't rankle. After all, who's the One they're naming anyway? And who's the One who cares? Still, wouldn't it be cool to be called something like Eternal Vortex of Eccentric Joy?

Or really, just nothing at all?

A World without You

Be in this world but not of it.
—Jesus of Nazareth

*There has never been a time when you and I have not
existed, nor will there be a time when we will cease to
be. Therefore play the role you're meant for right now.*
—Bhagavad Gita

Every yoga practice ends with *shavasana*, the corpse pose.
Laura, one of my teachers, always says it's the most advanced of all, complete detachment from this world, unclenching the spirit and the mind.

The other day in her class we all entered shavasana
as usual, lying flat on our backs, eyes closed, palms to the
sky. I could hear the drone of Oakland traffic. An ambulance screeched by. Some hip-hop blared for a moment and
subsided. The smell of fresh rolls from the bakery below
wafted up.

As we drifted into deep relaxation Laura said, "Imagine

that you have already left this planet. And imagine that the world goes on without you perfectly. All is well."

I had already experienced this during that long stretch in the eighties when I was ill. Unable to work, walk, or even think straight, I was dead to this world without being fully gone.

Though I eventually healed, the experience completely altered my being.

Before, I thought—like a true Capricorn with four Saturn squares—that work was my raison d'être. In fact my overexertion probably spawned the whole mess. Desperately needing to be liked, well-regarded, and most of all, to matter, I worked night and day.

But once my collapse came, I eerily saw the world continue quite well. And when I recovered in 1990 I was transformed. *Nothing* mattered as before. Seeing how easily I could be replaced or forgotten had been an odd gift and revelation.

Once I returned from the underworld, I couldn't believe my incredible good luck just to eat a bowl of coconut soup in a Thai cafe or walk on a windy beach.

The wonder never went away.

*It's good to know both your specialness and your
    utter dispensability.
Then you can let go and embrace it all.*

You can play your role in this exquisite, absurd
     story
with complete abandon.
You can be a melting snowflake, a drifting leaf, or
     a nature spirit
dancing in a pond.
And if you touch any heart with what you do
for the brief moments you are here,
that is enough.

Chapter Sixteen

BE WHAT THE WORLD NEEDS

Hate Therapy

*The problem was not our torturers but that we
began to hate them. Then we would be lost.*
—Thich Nhat Hanh

I was sitting in a Tribeca café when a guy walked in the
door, caught my eye, and strode over.

"Well, well, well, Gloria," he began, his voice shaking
with anger. "Look what the cat dragged in. I *knew* you'd
eventually get thrown my way. And what the hell did you
think would happen when I got that notice from your nut-
job ass-hat lawyer? Did you think that low-rent slimeball
could scare me into more dough?"

He went on for a few more loud, obscenity-laced minutes, while the writer in me sat riveted, musing, *"God, I miss New York!"*

Soon the nearby tables were listening and watching as I silently took off my sunglasses to reveal that no, actually I *wasn't* the guy's long-detested ex-wife.

Just a really, really close proxy.

He was so rattled he backed out the door as if he'd seen a ghost.

"Christ, you even *dress* like her," he mumbled as he left, staring at the floor. "Even the damn Mephisto sandals. Hey, sorry, lady. Really sorry."

This guy was such a great lesson. He'd been almost entertaining, since his rant had nothing to do with "me." Nothing personal.

But isn't a lot of anger that way? Someone might really be screaming without knowing it about that time they were left in the shopping cart at Safeway when they were three.

I once felt "venom at first sight" from another guy in a spiritual group where I belonged. Somehow the minute we met it kicked in for him.

One night I longed to pray for the poor guy, figuring he could use some help. He didn't exactly seem like the happiest person. Anyway, I had nothing to lose. I lit a green candle and sent him love and joy almost nightly.

About a month later he lumbered up. He half-growled, "Hey, I gotta tell ya. You used to bug the crap out of me.

And *now* I'm mad cuz I'm *not* mad. I don't know what the heck you're doin' but I don't hate ya." And he walked away.

We never spoke again, but that was enough.

Sometimes the people with the most anger need the most help. *You never know what sending them blessings may do.* You might be the only one on the planet winging good their way.

You never know.

To Catch a Thief

Upon being established in non-stealing, there
occurs the attainment of all prosperity.
—Patanjali Yoga Sutras ii:37

I've written a lot about Divine Source, the knowledge that all prosperity and good comes from God, not any individual person or job. Once you know how to tap this Source, you trust that what is meant for you will come in an organic way. It's a completely learnable skill.

A well-known author called me for a reading once. She said she picked me when she heard from someone that I wasn't particularly impressed by fame. I admitted that with four planets in egalitarian-minded Aquarius, that was pretty true.

Everyone is a chart to me, a colorful expression of God at the costume ball, all dressed up and pretending to be human. Maybe that's just what happens after a zillion readings. And anyway, I'd seen up close how money and power alone brought little contentment, no matter what this nutty culture claimed.

Well, the writer was calling to confess. While she had made a fortune with her books, she knew she had stolen her work, lifting them from a humble self-published tome years before. She had never reached the guy for permission or acknowledged him in any way.

Now here's the kicker. While the original author never came after her, this woman lived in scarcity and fear despite her vast success. If she had two houses, she wanted three. If she was on one talk show, she wanted ten. She lived in a state of perpetual, restless, roaming greed like an itinerant hungry ghost. Her stealing had locked her into a prison of lack.

I suggested she finally reach the man, who still lived in nearby El Cerrito, to make serious amends and restitution. She was relieved at the thought.

Her karma would have to be reversed before she could ever feel abundant, no matter *how* much she owned.

The Wayward Yogini

*I have unshakeable faith in the perfect outcome of
every situation in my life, for I am allowing God to be
in absolute control and guide me in all proper actions.*
—Catherine Ponder

Last Thanksgiving, I heard from Maura, a local yoga teacher who was terrified because her classes were shrinking. She wanted to know why.

As we talked it got apparent. She constantly calculated the number of students she would need to pay her bills. She saw herself in anxious competition with any other teacher. And she envisioned a diminishing pool of potential private sessions as money got tighter in the current economy. With rising fear, she tried to constantly corral and manipulate new folks to pay her bills. Yet when folks felt her grasping, they understandably fled.

In short, she had one major problem. She had turned each potential student into her Source.

But there's a whole other way.

"What if you saw yourself as lucky to have work that relieves suffering?" I asked. "What if your 'bottom line' belonged to God, and your only role was to serve with as much love as possible?"

"You mean do my classes for free?" she scoffed. "What about my bills?"

"No, no, you can charge." I continued, "but if you shift your energy *out* of your lower survival chakras, and move into your heart, a miracle will come. If you see the Divine as your Source, the funds can arrive from wherever It picks. You could apply this to any livelihood, but jeez, you're teaching yoga! How the heck can you leave God out of the equation?"

"And anyway," I went on. "There's no such *thing* as competition. You attract people by your own nature. The people who are drawn to your particular energy will always find you. You don't have to worry if there's a yoga studio on every block."

Maura grimaced. "Well, in Berkeley there actually *is*."

"Yeh, but no one else is YOU."

So she prayed steadily for the next few weeks,

I'm now available to receive anyone who can benefit from my teaching. Let all who need me find me. Let me help relieve suffering. The Divine is my complete Source for all prosperity and will provide.

As she released her grasp, her classes started filling once more. She also began offering some free ones to those in need.

And she remembered why on earth she had been drawn to teach yoga in the first place.

Why Please Everyone?

Release the noose of public opinion.
> —Lori Anders

The only sin is to have knowledge that
could assist others, and to hoard it.
> —Anonymous

I've been giving readings to Sosa forever. She's based in Montana, isolated from the urban art world. She recently did her first big show in Los Angeles, and overnight people were clamoring for more. Suddenly with the internet, she saw that her work could travel the globe.

She's also got a Herculean birth chart with a prominent Pluto, the planet of death and rebirth, kicking up dirt wherever she goes. People instantly adore her or hate her. Her energy is so strong, she changes a room just by walking in the door.

None of this would matter except she also has three planets in sensitive Libra that are mortified each time she attracts even a flicker of dislike.

She called because she felt uncomfortable promoting herself on the web. I knew what she meant. I'd rather get three root canals in one day than do the kind of hard-sell promotion many marketers advise. Much of it just makes my stomach hurt.

But there's another way.

If you trust that you have something of value to offer, you *want* to tell people as an act of love. In fact, if you have something that can benefit them, it can even be misguided selfishness to *not* share.

~~~

The other day I flashed on Sosa's soul painted in bold, jewel-like colors, like the hues of Mexico or South America where she's often gone. Vivid turquoise, fuchsia, purple, gold. But then there's her cautious Libra always muting everything, hoping to create inoffensive, soft, delicate pastels.

Well, this chick is sooo totally not pastel.

Sosa's work genuinely rocks people to their core, but she had a false, useless modesty that kept the world from knowing. I suggested she make her website, do some social networking, and let her ship set sail.

She could say:

*I call Divine Order into my work. In the right time,
in the right way, let my offering become available*

for the good of all, to all who need to be guided to
me and to know.

If she centered in her heart and used Divine Order to beckon
and invite those who needed her, they would surely come.

There are charts that are restrained and delightful, like
small clay pots of perfect violets on a sunny window ledge.
But Sosa's energy was *meant* to be larger than life, a flamboyant and reckless bird of paradise arcing toward the sun.

And when she owns her true energy, the earth itself will
breathe a long, deep sigh . . . of relief.

~~

Something happens after you align with the Divine for a while.

You begin to feel on a cellular level
that things are unfolding exactly
in the way that they should.
At the rate and timing they need.

You start to trust the process.

You relax from the endless pushing
that most of us learned at birth.
On some fundamental, mysterious level,
you just let go.

Not with that bitterness people feel
when they fear the (ego's) dreams won't occur.
Not with passivity
as right actions do get shown.

Rather you relax into this calm curiosity
about where the flow might go.
You're detached yet somehow riveted
by how the story will unfold.
You feel spaciously receptive
and open to what wishes to come.

You give it all room to blossom.
You trust the highest,
one way or another,
eventually will unfold.

You know that with God as your Source
you needn't cling to any one plan
And you're not clutching a list of desires,
pushing the ego's agenda even more.

When you're in cycles of quiet and waiting,
you catch your breath
knowing the wheel again will turn.

You rest because as the right actions
get revealed
a lot will arise to be done.
You wait for the signs and the timing
rather than rip open the cocoon.

You trust that delays might be welcome.
You trust that delays can be good.
You trust that delays are all perfect.

And you stay present
just to witness

your own birth.

Acknowledgments

I had no idea about the adventures (and challenges) that would unfold in my life once my columns at SF Examiner .com morphed into a book. Luckily, the Divine sent more assistance than I could have ever imagined. This work would simply not exist without certain people.

Alice Turkel was my steady phone companion, Capricorn alter ego, peripatetic editor, advisor, healer, and cheerleader. She towed this stuck car out of so many snow banks, I will never be able to thank her enough. She is my dearest friend and sister.

Dr. Christiane Northrup was the Guardian Angel of this book in more ways than could ever be said. A true Kaliesque soul sister.

Dr. Lissa Rankin changed my life as soon as we met and I feel lucky to be her friend. Every day I am inspired by her courage, intelligence, and beautiful heart. I also will never be able to hike as fast as her, no matter how I try.

Matthew Klein arrived in response to deep prayers I didn't even know I had made. He has turned out to be the perfect manager and guide for my work. I am grateful every day for his generosity, vision, and insanely quick wit.

And thank you to Johanna Castillo, my editor at Atria Books for "getting" what this book is about from the very first phone call. You arrived on my mother's birthday, and I know she sent you. You are a true gift.

Stephanie Tade has been the best agent imaginable. She is kindhearted, spiritual, and a sublime businesswoman all at once.

Heather Mahan has been my most blessed assistant, neighbor, and kick-ass Resident Cat Goddess. Plus, she just makes me laugh, almost every day.

Cheela "Rome" Smith, drag king and artiste extraordinaire, made the rockin' cover and made me laugh. Constantly.

Donna Insalaco took the picture on the back cover with her blend of bighearted, badass New York–Italian creative fire.

Celeste Gray in North Carolina was an insightful editor of the first edition who helped finalize its structure.

Michael Fantasia arrived, thank God, with the fabulous skills to turn the original edition of *Outrageous Openness* into a "real" book.

Sarah Buscho has been my beloved baby sister, holding my hand through challenges of every kind.

Kaiel Kaliber has not only been a great support, she's also been the sake-boy par excellence at every damn book party we gave.

Also a deep bow to the Facebook tribe that arose on my author page after the original edition of *Outrageous Openness*. Their love, support, and wacky laughter have truly sustained me. I've spent almost every morning of the last three years writing with them. I love you all.

Finally, thank you to my brother, Michael, who once said, "I always knew you were a writer. I just wondered if you'd be the last one to find out."

And to the *San Francisco Examiner* for making me find out.

And to Florence Scovel Shinn for gettin' the party started.

And to Nisargadatta Maharaj, Bhagawan Nityananda, and Adyashanti for keeping me glued to Reality.

Most of all, I bow in complete gratitude to that Divine and Holy Power that animates All, the Supreme Shakti Herself, endlessly enchanting, luring, and captivating me.

~~

I am Yours.

Ten questions from readers about <u>Outrageous Openness</u>

1. I love the title. Where did it come from?

True story. Back in 2011 the book originally was going to be called *Outrageous Optimism*. But then two days before self-publishing it, I discovered that another book with the same title already existed.

I put panic aside and did exactly what *Outrageous Openness* would say. I offered to the Divine that the perfect name was already selected and would arise in the right way. I felt a warm calm within me. Later that day, I decided to go for a pedicure. For some crazy reason, I knew I would get a sign there.

As I was picking the color at the salon, I was drawn to a bright turquoise which was called "Be Open." And that was it!

This is proof that the Divine can even use a random pedicure, or any other experience, to bring you the right answer. The Divine just wants to be included.

2. How is this different from focusing on Law of Attraction and manifesting?

It's a very different focus, although parts of Law of Attraction are included in *Outrageous Openness*. For example, our thoughts do impact our reality. If we constantly think negative or fearful thoughts, we will invariably attract those experiences. Keeping a high vibe is a key part of this book.

I find that focusing on manifesting is limited and exhausting, since it leaves God out. It often involves a shopping list of what the ego wants to "get from the universe." By its very nature that's profoundly limited. A friend even wrote a funny story once called "Now that I manifested it, how the heck do I get RID of it?" Not every desire is for our highest good!

Outrageous Openness is about allowing for intimacy with the Divine. Since this force of Love knows our heart and soul completely, deep desires often are fulfilled in surprising ways as one learns to align with it. I like to always say "I myself don't manifest a darn thing. I actually have zero interest. I'd much rather see what God does through me." In *Outrageous Openness*, you will learn how to offer your problems to the Divine and *get out of the way* so what's meant to happen, can happen. You can stop manipulating reality and allow the good to happen through you. You can invite this Force of Love to *use* you. The more you ask to be a vehicle for the highest force, the more that it will occur.

3. I liked your book but I'm very focused on co-creation. I tell God what I want and then we work on it together. How is that different?

After working with thousands of people over the years, I've found that most folks view co-creation as telling God how to get what they (the ego) want. I want this Force of Love to use ME, not the other way around. It's not that desires go away, but they become preferences that are offered over. This is very different from *using* God in service to the ego.

If I have a specific need, I'll say "The perfect answer is already picked and I'll be shown the right way and time according to God's will." That also leaves room for Divine Love to say "No, you don't need that right now!" Because that's what letting Love lead is all about. Offering, offering, and offering.

4. If I don't tell God what I need, how will It know? Don't I need to make specific vision boards so the Universe doesn't get confused?

God. Made. You! Are you kidding? Now that I live this way, I'm always astonished how the Divine brings even the smallest things I didn't know I even *wanted or needed*, until they arrive. And I always think, oh my goodness, *How oh how did you know?*

5. Don't you want your wishes to come true?

I want God's wishes for me to come true. My own wishes, especially in my twenties and thirties, created nothing but a trail of wreckage and heartbreak. There's a reason that twelve-step programs talk about "Self-Will Run Riot." I was the poster child.

Offering wishes to the Divine allows them to be fulfilled, delayed, or ignored. Wishes and desires then become preferences. This brings detachment from your desires, space, and peace. You truly stop being a slave to obsessions. Things will often arrive in ways you never imagined, because your detachment has actually allowed room for a Higher Plan to emerge. This brings pure and simple happiness.

6. Well, I believe God helps those who help themselves. How is letting the Divine take the Lead not just passivity and lying around?

I get this question so often I once wrote a blog post called "Why Letting the Divine Take the Lead has NOTHING to Do with Doing Nothing." Because our culture is so dualistic by nature, the focus is either on "make it happen" or "be passive." But trusting the Divine is neither. Letting the Divine take the lead is about offering problems (including one's whole life!) over and then allowing the right actions to arise at the right time. You start to know when to wait . . .

and when to act. Everything comes organically. You stop wasting time doing something when it's not yet ripe. You learn how to go with the green lights. You learn how to wait. The more you invite in this approach, the easier it gets. *Outrageous Openness* describes how to do it quite thoroughly.

7. What would you say to someone who doesn't believe that there is a Divine in the first place?

I've gotten thousands of letters over the last two years since *Outrageous Openness* first came out, and some of my favorites are from atheists and agnostics. You really don't have to believe in a conventional idea of God for these ideas to bear fruit. Many people who were turned off by traditional religion have made their way back to harmony with a Force greater than the ego through this book. Even if you just engage with the idea of "Love" or "The Force that Lets Bird Fly" that's enough. You can practice offering to that. You can offer to Your Own Wisest Self too. That works. Why not just try it as an experiment?

8. What are the simplest ways to begin? I'm overwhelmed by the need to change.

There are very simple tools. For example, read chapter four on the God Box and get one. This is a box where you offer over concerns and worries to the Divine. You allow the burden to be cast to God and you release the idea that it belongs to "you." For most people, that's the perfect starting point.

Also, just open the book anywhere. You don't have to read it cover to cover at first. Just ask it a question and see what it answers.

You can also pray: "Open me, Divine, to what I need to know right now. Allow me to open to the changes you wish for me." Or make up your own. *Outrageous Openness* is all about inviting in the energy of engagement and intimacy. It's not about following rules like in so many spiritual courses and books.

9. Does Letting the Divine Take the Lead mean that every day becomes a full-time happy party?

Definitely not. I have challenging days and stretches like anyone else. The only difference is, I constantly invite Divine help all day long. It's become second nature now, and it changes everything. A larger energy guides all. Luckily, anyone can learn to do this.

10. What does it mean to be Outrageously Open?

When the agendas and shopping lists of the ego are released, room is created for a Divine Plan far beyond the manipulations of the mind. To me, this is what creates true happiness and awakening. Then existence becomes a daily surprise as it unfolds, and we can literally be used by Love as a force for good. Life happens through us and for us, rather than BY us. It is actually a very, very powerful way to live. And it is available to anyone . . . with practice.

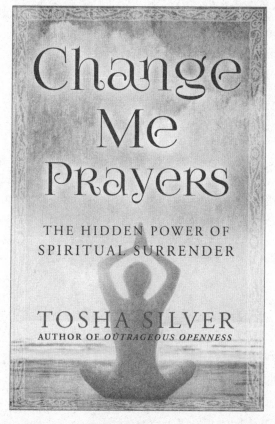